RILKE'S
Book of
HOURS

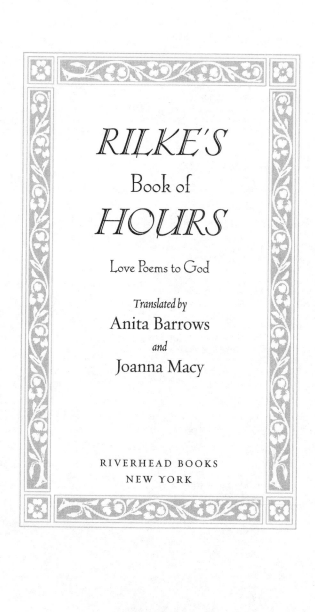

RILKE'S
Book of
HOURS

Love Poems to God

Translated by
Anita Barrows
and
Joanna Macy

RIVERHEAD BOOKS
NEW YORK

RIVERHEAD BOOKS
Published by the Penguin Group
Penguin Group (USA) Inc.
375 Hudson Street, New York, New York 10014, USA
Penguin Group (Canada), 90 Eglinton Avenue East, Suite 700, Toronto, Ontario M4P 2Y3, Canada
(a division of Pearson Penguin Canada Inc.)
Penguin Books Ltd., 80 Strand, London WC2R 0RL, England
Penguin Group Ireland, 25 St. Stephen's Green, Dublin 2, Ireland (a division of Penguin Books Ltd.)
Penguin Group (Australia), 250 Camberwell Road, Camberwell, Victoria 3124, Australia
(a division of Pearson Australia Group Pty. Ltd.)
Penguin Books India Pvt. Ltd., 11 Community Centre, Panchsheel Park, New Delhi—110 017, India
Penguin Group (NZ), 67 Apollo Drive, Rosedale, North Shore 0632, New Zealand
(a division of Pearson New Zealand Ltd.)
Penguin Books (South Africa) (Pty.) Ltd., 24 Sturdee Avenue, Rosebank, Johannesburg 2196,
South Africa

Penguin Books Ltd., Registered Offices: 80 Strand, London WC2R 0RL, England

The publisher does not have any control over and does not assume any responsibility for author or third-party websites or their content.

First Riverhead hardcover edition: March 1996
First Riverhead trade paperback edition: April 1997
First Riverhead revised trade paperback edition: November 2005

Library of Congress Cataloging-in-Publication Data

Rilke, Rainer Maria, 1875–1926.
    {Stundenbuch. English & German}
    Rilke's Book of hours : love poems to God / translated by Anita Barrows and Joanna
Macy.—1st Riverhead rev. trade pbk. ed
        p. cm.
    English and German.
    ISBN 978-1-59448-156-7
        I. Title: Book of hours. II. Barrows, Anita. III. Macy, Joanna, 1929- IV. Title.

PT2635.I65S72513 2005
831'.912—dc22

                                                                                    2005044352

PRINTED IN THE UNITED STATES OF AMERICA

33rd Printing

I am the one whose praise echoes on high.
I adorn all the earth.
I am the breeze that nurtures all things green.
I encourage blossoms to flourish with ripening fruits.
I am led by the spirit to feed the purest streams.
I am the rain coming from the dew
that causes the grasses to laugh with the joy of life.
I am the yearning for good.

HILDEGARD VON BINGEN

Contents

Acknowledgments

This new, expanded edition of Rilke's *Book of Hours* carries our wholehearted thanks to the many people who, over the last ten years, have loved these poems and taken them into their lives. Cherishing these poems as we do, nothing could be more gratifying to us than to have our rendering of them so widely welcomed and used. They have been spoken and sung in weddings and funerals, political gatherings and environmental actions. To our delight they have inspired composers, choreographers, and filmmakers. And now they have inspired this centenary publication, which happily includes the German originals.

RILKE'S
Book of
HOURS

.

Preface

JOANNA MACY

For almost fifty years, since the winter's day I found it on a table in a Munich bookstore, Rainer Maria Rilke's *Book of Hours* has been a cherished companion. My book is the original Insel Verlag edition, clothbound, with Gothic script on soft rag paper, and on the cover the print of the three-jetted fountain the poet had chosen. This pocket-size volume has traveled with me across the spiritual landscapes of my life—from the rubble of a once-sturdy faith in church and God, into the streets of political activism, and into the Buddha-fields of South and Central Asia.

The first poem I recall reading was as exhilarating to me as the fresh cold alpine wind off the slopes I loved to ski:

I live my life in widening circles
that reach out across the world.
I may not ever complete the last one,
but I give myself to it.

I circle around God, that primordial tower.
I have been circling for thousands of years,
and I still don't know: am I a falcon,
a storm, or a great song?   [I, 2]

I felt a sense of release, as if I had been let out of a cage I had not known I was in. Rilke's images lent some pattern, even meaning, to a life I thought had failed in its spiritual vocation. Once I had imagined that my journey would be like the Pilgrim's Progress, where each adventure brings the hero closer to the heavenly city, but the Christian God with whom I had been intoxicated in my teenage years did not survive the theological studies I undertook to serve him (and it was a him). When I turned outward, angry and heartsick, to political affairs, I found that I was a failure as an atheist, too, for I could not cure myself of praying to a God I no longer believed in.

Now those same lines, read for the first time on a snow-packed Munich street, shed a new light on the patchwork my life had become—marriage, motherhood, abandoned government career, assortment of jobs, studies in art and language. Perhaps, after all, some unknowable center held me in orbit. Rilke reminded me that if my spiritual appetite was greater than the tedious, cramped theorizing of the theologians, so was God. I could almost feel again the sense of belonging and purpose that I thought I had forfeited.

The Book of Hours came with me to Asia, eight years later, when I went to live in India with my young family and the Peace Corps. There, through work with Tibetan refugees, Buddhism entered my life and brought a sense of ease and strength in the patterns it revealed for structuring experience—patterns that seemed familiar. Rilke, in *The Book of Hours*, had expressed the sacred in terms and images I now found central to Buddhist teachings, concepts such as "law" and "way" (*"du sanftestes Gesetz ..."*) and images of wheel and net ("You are a wheel at which I stand"; "you dark net threading through us").

When I first undertook meditative practice, I did not feel a divine presence, an encompassing Other to be held and supported by, which seemed to be there for the young Rilke.

> *Don't you sense me, ready to break*
> *into being at your touch?*   [I, 19]

But gradually over time, as the mind relaxed, capacities bred by my earlier Christian experience resurfaced and infused my understanding of Buddhism. The presence that I became aware of, around and within me, is apprehended through an act of rapt, wordless attention, receptive and probing. And what the presence seems to *be* is the web itself, the thrumming relationality of all things.

Rilke's recognition of the reciprocal nature of our relationship with God, and even with life, is itself a poetic and profoundly personal complement to the Buddha's central doctrine of dependent co-arising. Asserting the radical interdependence at the core of existence, this teaching seemed to me at times a bit abstract, so I loved reading again: "What will you do, God, when I die?" (I, 36).

This sense of reciprocity nourished my engagement in work for social change, and was fed by it in turn. There came a time in the middle and late 1970s when the enormity of what I was discovering as an environmental activist—especially about the widespread, long-term, devastating effects of nuclear weapons production—broke through my defenses. I struggled simply to take in what was happening to our world, and to sustain the gaze long enough to be of use. Rilke's unwhining acceptance of the fact that, yes, a world can die, strengthened me in its straightforwardness and lack of self-pity.

I found that many of my colleagues and fellow citizens were silently suffering and suppressing a similar anguish. Buddhist teachings and my Judeo-Christian roots helped me understand this pain for the world. Rilke helped, too.

You are not surprised at the force of the storm— you have seen it growing. . . .

Now you must go out into your heart as onto a vast plain. Now the immense loneliness begins. . . .

Through the empty branches the sky remains. It is what you have.   [II, 1]

Those lines murmured like mantras in my mind. I felt Rilke helping me face this time of terror and promise, as I moved out into the public arena with a form of group work based explicitly on the extent and depth of our social despair.

Lord, the great cities are lost and rotting.
Their time is running out. [III, 4]

The work I found myself doing helped people overcome denial about the condition of our world. It taught me that understanding our despair, and not shrinking from it, transforms it into strong, connective energy.

That your world is in agony is no reason to turn your back on it, or to try to escape into private "spiritual" pursuits. Rilke reminded me that I had the strength and courage to walk out into the world as into my own heart, and to "love the things / as no one has thought to love them" (I, 61).

My own stubborn, wild love for the world was summoned, and I learned to recognize it in others, too, in the movements for peace, global justice, and ecological sanity. Rilke confirmed my sense of a deep passion at the core of life itself, which I could come home to, the way sheep come home at nightfall, "the dark bridge thudding" (I, 40). I could die into that passion, as into a lover's arms, trusting its ongoingness and its vast sufficient intelligence.

With Rilke I came to see that intelligence—the "play of the powers"—in the simplest of things, to take comfort in the texture of bark, the acorn's gleaming body, the leaping squirrel. The poet's images of web and wheel, of root and branch, reminded me how the things connect, in interwoven patterns and mutual belonging.

> *Your wholeness cascades into many shapes.*
> *You run like a herd of luminous deer*
> *and I am dark, I am forest.*   [I, 45]

Rilke never said that the path to political empowerment lay through darkness, he just said God was there. But he bolstered my conviction that we must go that way in order to break out of denial. Only then can the "play of the powers," the intelligence of life, work through us, so to heal a broken world.

Naturally, over the years, I wanted to share *The Book of Hours* with my friends. I searched in vain for English translations that conveyed their brave, luminous simplicity. Sometimes, in spells of sadness or dryness, when I wanted to enter the poems more deeply, I tried my hand at translating them myself. I knew what I was seeking, but I was frustrated by my attempt to hold on to meter and rhyme, which made my efforts in English sound trite.

Then, in 1993, I began again, with my friend Anita Barrows, an accomplished poet. We began with the poem I had most wanted to share with my fellow activists who don't read German. It was the first poem of the second cycle, *"Dich wundert nicht des Sturmes Wucht."* Then, after that, we kept on for the sheer pleasure of it. We had no idea that we had embarked on a book, and on one of the most joyous adventures of our lives.

Preface

ANITA BARROWS

I knew nothing of the poems in Rilke's *Book of Hours* until the evening in May 1993 when Joanna Macy read to me, in German, the two that would initiate our work, "You are not surprised at the force of the storm" and "What will you do, God, when I die?" The second, in its affirmation of God's need for us, seemed very close to a thought that had accompanied me in childhood. Brought up as I was in a highly patriarchal Jewish family—both my grandfathers had been Orthodox rabbis, one in Poland and the other in Hungary—I was steeped in an image of a God who was anything but dependent. Jealous, hot-tempered, the Yahweh I intuited from those around me was a huge, remote eye in the sky watching and waiting for us to falter and fail him.

What could I feel except fear before such a punitive God? And yet one Saturday in autumn when I was about six, trailing after my father on the walk home from Sabbath services, I understood something new about God. There on the boulevard, amid the noise and bustle of Brooklyn, was this delicious mulching smell, this crispness, this crackling noise of dry red and yellow leaves. The smell awakened me after the morning spent in the dim, drafty synagogue, where I had to sit upstairs listening to the men chanting below in a language I did not understand. *God made these leaves, this smell*, I said to myself, and suddenly it occurred to me that God created the world because he was lonely. He needed it—needed the ripeness of autumn, the bright air, the sunlight making patterns on the sidewalk through linden leaves that were yet unfallen. God had created all this, and us as well, to keep him company. That far, chilly place where he lived had felt empty to him without our world. The idea seemed so blasphemous to me that I dared not speak it, but I found it both exciting and comforting.

Rilke's poem of the great oncoming storm spoke to me of the repeated moments in my life when I had departed from what was known and familiar—a place, a group, a belief, a partner—to follow something that compelled me from what seemed a place of deep instinctual knowing. "Now you must go out into your heart / as onto a vast plain," Rilke wrote.

I left the synagogue at sixteen in search of something that felt more akin to the God revealed to me under the linden leaves, and less like the father "in king's robes," with "scepter and crown," as Rilke describes the images of God he, too, resisted. Coming west from New York at nineteen, I experienced in the vast, dramatic geography of California the same awe I had felt in the presence of Yahweh, with none of the remoteness. Nature became what was holy for me: the silence of redwoods, the granite peaks of the northern Sierra, the desert. For a long time I did not want to speak about God.

Then, during my graduate student days, my study of medieval Italian literature, especially Dante, drew me to Catholicism, with its incarnate God who loved and suffered humanly. I took instruction in the Church and was baptized. Week after week I received the Eucharist and found great joy in it; but I could not get over feeling like an impostor. My Jewishness would not let me give myself fully to Christian forms and rituals, and anyway, it was the spare medieval monastery I longed for and not the institutional Church. After a time I returned to a meditative practice I had been doing on and off for years, without naming it religion; eventually it was an open, nonsectarian Buddhism that I embraced.

In the spring of 1993, when Joanna and I began working with *The Book of Hours*, I was completing a long poem of my own, which I called *A Record*. I was weaving together images from the Jewish Holocaust with images of the suffering of other peoples and species, the suffering of our earth. The poem grew from my utter conviction of the interconnectedness of all these forms of suffering. I did not intend to trivialize any particular suffering by setting it alongside others; but some of my Jewish friends criticized the poem for doing just that. How could I speak of the dying of frogs and the incineration of Jews in the same breath? Inner voices judged me as well; as a Jewish child born only two years after the liberation of the concentration camps, I grew up steeped in stories of Nazi atrocities. Was I minimizing my people's pain by placing it in context with other pain? And yet I knew, from the ways in which my heart kept breaking over the genocide of other peoples as well as the dying of frogs and the poisoning of the seas, that for these, too, a holocaust was occurring, and I had no choice but to name it.

> *Be modest now, like a thing*
> *ripened until it is real,*
> *so that he who began it all*
> *can feel you when he reaches for you.*   [II, 1]

Rilke's summons to the journey into his own heart helped me find the courage to continue writing A Record. It helped me, as well, to put into perspective my own doubt about what I was doing and how my friends and colleagues might judge it. Reading these words, it was a relief to see myself just as one bit of God's creation, no more exalted than a branch, a stone, or a drop of water. Rilke's sense of a God who could reach for me in my barest simplicity—in my most "real" and "ripened" self—pleased me.

Reading Rilke again also brought back to me my own beginnings as a poet. In 1964, when I was seventeen, I was invited to spend a week on Cape Cod with a friend whose parents were German. On the long drive up from New York, my friend's father, a writer, recited by heart one after another of Rilke's *Sonnets to Orpheus*—first in German, then in his own elegant impromptu translation. Imagine the fire kindled in me! When, months later, I tentatively brought to my friend's Manhattan apartment a notebook filled with sonnets of my own, her father's first response after reading them was to go to his shelf and pull out a copy of Rilke's *Letters to a Young Poet*. "If you are going to be a poet you must read Rilke," he told me, and gave me the volume to keep. "Rilke is the poet's poet." The letters went everywhere with me for years, along with *The Notebooks of Malte Laurids Brigge*, which I read shortly afterward. It would not be an exaggeration to say that those two books shaped and concentrated for me my vocation as a poet, and when I signed up for a German class in my second year of college, it was with the express purpose of reading Rilke in the original.

When Joanna and I started working—or, actually, playing—with those first two poems, I had not translated anything for a long time, even though I had worked professionally as a translator for ten years before I trained as a psychologist. On my early-morning walks in those weeks after we began, I found myself obsessively turning phrases in my head, and remembered the joy I had experienced in translation—different from the act of writing my own poetry, yet similar. This playful experiment with Rilke's early poems was answering some very deep longing within me. It was a complex longing, born of delight in language, yes, but also of the isolation of being a poet—isolation precisely in moments of the purest fulfillment my life knew. To share this process, this intimate space, with another person seemed an incredible privilege. It made me quiver with happiness, and also a little apprehension. It was hard to believe, at first, that poetic creativity could really be shared. Apprehension quickly yielded to exhilaration.

As Joanna and I allowed these poems to reveal their meanings to us, I discovered still deeper resonances between them and the most pervasive themes of my life. Rilke's love for things of this world, his insistence that they—we—are what is sacred, his capacity to see the holy in the ordinary—all these had informed my own poetry from the start.

I know that nothing has ever been real without my beholding it.
All becoming has needed me.
My looking ripens things
and they come toward me, to meet and be met. [I, I]

A person (or a thing) comes to exist by being met in the most authentic way by another. My practice of psychotherapy has been deeply informed by the Jungian principle of reciprocal individuation, which means that a deep and loving encounter is what generates development.

How close this is to Rilke's declaration that our greatest summons is really to see the things of this world. We *are* because we are seen; we *are* because we are loved. The world *is* because it is beheld and loved into being. On a silent retreat, while watching a line of ants traveling up a hillside, words came to me that I would repeat again and again in my mind: *I am in the world to love the world.* I knew, standing there in the parched summer grasses, how deeply the poems of *The Book of Hours* had already penetrated my being, speaking to me as instructions for living.

Introduction

This volume celebrates the hundredth anniversary of what has come to be recognized as a major literary event. In December 1905, the Insel Verlag of Leipzig published a collection of poems that had been kept private, read only by the woman to whom they were dedicated. Although the young Rainer Maria Rilke was in the habit of disseminating his verses widely, this particular set of poems—135 in all—had been assiduously kept from the public eye. To him, they were as personal as prayers, and that is what he called them, *Gebete*. Yet these very prayers, once published and welcomed as *Das Stunden-Buch (The Book of Hours)*, constituted the work that Rilke would claim as the true commencement of his poetic legacy.

The young Rilke had written the poems that would make up *The Book of Hours* in three brief, intense periods of inspiration between 1899 and 1903. When he began, he was twenty-three years old and had already published three volumes of poetry. By late 1905, when *The Book of Hours* was published, Rilke had written several of the prose works for which he is best known, including *The Lay of the Love and Death of Cornet Christopher Rilke* and a series of letters to Franz Kappus, which would be collected under the title *Letters to a Young Poet*.

The impulse that ignited the poems, as Rilke wrote to Marlise Gerding in May 1911, came after a period during which he received what he called "inner dictations," words that came to him mornings and evenings and that struck him with their force and persistence. The process of writing, as Rilke told Gerding, strengthened and stimulated the inspiration, and he realized that a genuine work had been initiated.

But the poems that came forth—like the poems that were to follow in 1901 and 1903—were felt to be too intimate, too sacred even, for publication. Unmentioned in his letters and even in his journal, these were placed only in the hands of his beloved Lou Andreas-Salomé. *"Gelegt in die Hände von Lou,"* he wrote in dedication when preparing the final manuscript. He chose the title then, inspired by the French medieval tradition of *livres d'heures*, devotional breviaries for lay use.

Rilke's Early Life

The poet was born on December 4, 1875, in Prague, then a provincial capital in the Austro-Hungarian Empire, and christened René Karl Wilhelm Johann Josef Maria Rilke. His parents' limited means made them all the more conscious of their social status as members of Prague's small German-speaking elite. In their pretentious, insular world he had, he said, "an anxious, heavy childhood."

An only child, René endured the sentimental upbringing of a mother who still grieved the loss of her baby daughter, and who brought him up as a girl until he was six years old. Increasingly unhappy in her marriage, she took him into churches to pray with her and, as he would later recall with distaste, kiss Christ's wounds on the crucifix. At home she spent long private hours playing with him and dressing him "like a big doll." His father, a stiff, uncommunicative man, was a railroad official who had served as a cadet in the emperor's army, and still grieved the loss of his military career. For his son, the elder Rilke mandated military school.

At ten years old, in prescribed uniform and haircut, René found himself abandoned to an emotionally repressive, loudly regulated, hypermasculine world. He cooperated as well as he could, but his five years there were hateful to him. Even thirty years later, he would characterize that experience as carrying for him "the feeling of one single terrible damnation." Teased by the other boys, he was agonizingly lonely, but the cruelest thing was the crowding of the mind in the close quarters, with constantly interrupting commands, bullying, and competition—from which he found relief only in the relative silence and solitude of the infirmary.

Poetry was a refuge for him there, and when ill health finally won him his release from the military academy, poetry shaped the student life into which he threw himself, in Linz and especially in Prague and Munich. Rilke's energy and versatility brought him friends and recognition in university literary circles. Something of a dandy, with his silver-headed cane and bowler hat, he found himself gifted with a strong capacity for relationship, particularly with women, and eager for the discoveries and disclosures these relationships allowed. He adopted easily the romantic lyricism of his time, with its affectations and vaunting, facile subjectivity. Afire with creativity and enthusiastic about his own work, he was tireless in promoting it: not only with famous poets and writers of the period, whom he deluged with letters, but also with the populace at large, among whom he distributed a self-published journal free of charge.

Despite family pressures and expectations, Rilke knew he could not live his life other than as writer, as poet. Yet he was faced with the need to support himself economically, so this calling was hard to defend. He went through the motions of matriculating for a law degree, then for one in philosophy, but the urge to create, to bring to birth something new and necessary, made it impossible to follow through with anything resembling a conventional career. Without support from his family, he turned to others for the material help he needed in order to write, and took up what would become a lifelong burden: seeking a sponsor, an advance on future work, a suitable place to write, a grant or job to tide him through, over and over again explaining, justifying, promising, thanking. Already, however, he was able to point to considerable literary output, as poems, prose pieces, and plays appeared in journals and even on the stage.

The mature Rilke would dismiss the literary efforts of these early years. They surely served his poetic gifts by exercising them, but they embarrassed him later with their shallowness and their essentially imitative character. The soon-to-be-composed *Book of Hours*, although uncharacteristically kept secret for years, was the first work that the poet would acknowledge throughout his life as an authentic expression of his art and his being.

The Years that Brought Forth
The Book of Hours

While a student in Munich in 1897, far away from his mother's devout superstitions, René Rilke was drawn to sort through his own religious assumptions and attitudes. He sensed that there must be an authentic ground to the superstructures of his culture's faith, and in a deeply inward process that contrasted with his busy life in coffeehouses, literary salons, and editorial offices, he wanted to find it.

A long series of poems titled *Visions of Christ* presented a superfluous Jesus defeated and shamed by his arrogant attempt to interpose himself between humanity and God. These poems were not published until after Rilke's death, but he did send some to a writer he had not met, who had written an essay that he felt reflected a similar orientation. The essay was "Jesus the Jew," and the writer was Lou Andreas-Salomé.

A two-month sojourn in Tuscany drew Rilke into the world of Italian Renaissance religious art. Avidly he drank it in, exhilarated by the sensuous colors and forms and the warmly human portrayal of the divine. The unmannered tenderness of Fra Angelico and Botticelli conveyed an authentic, alluring devotion, and showed Rilke that the holy can be rooted in the body and in human relationship.

Lou Andreas-Salomé was a beautiful thirty-six-year-old Russian woman of strong intellect and independent character, born in St. Petersburg and living in a friendly, platonic marriage with an older German professor. When Rilke, at twenty-one, finally met her in a Munich salon in May 1897, she was already noted for her earlier liaison with Nietzsche. The young poet immediately pursued her with great determination, and they became lovers, in the most passionately fulfilling relationship either had yet known. Lou was the one woman Rilke would never cease loving, while he remained for her, as she later wrote, "the first true reality" in her life; they were "like brother and sister, but from primeval times before incest became a sacrilege." Their friendship, even after it stopped being sexual (at her discretion), was fundamental and generative to every aspect of the poet's development.

To begin with, he quieted down. His energies, scattered centrifugally in the frenzied, somewhat superficial life he had been leading, settled and deepened. Lou's own love of nature pulled him out of the city, out to walk barefoot through meadows and copses that now were real to him in their own right and not just a backdrop to his moods. Lou was at work on a book about Nietzsche, and the iconoclastic philosopher's thought provided a broader context for Rilke's own rebellion against the hypocrisies of conventional Christianity. Two changes in his life were emblematic of Lou's impact: he dropped, at her urging, the name *René* for the more masculine-sounding Germanic *Rainer*; and his handwriting was transformed into a more confident, elegant, and relaxed script.

In the spring of 1899, Rilke accompanied Lou and her husband to Russia and discovered the land and the spirituality that would so strongly imbue *The Book of Hours*—and his life. From there, he wrote his friend Frieda von Bülow:

> At bottom one seeks in everything new (country or person or thing) only an expression that helps some personal confession to greater power and maturity. All things are there in order that they may . . . become images for us. And they do not suffer from it, for while they are expressing us more and more clearly, our souls close over them in the same measure. And I feel in these days that Russian things will give me the names for those most timid devoutnesses of my nature which, since my childhood, have been longing to enter my art.

It is as though Rilke had been waiting for whatever in the world would correspond to feeling-states that had been constellating inside him, and he found it in Russia—in the living forms of communal worship he witnessed there, and also in landscape and architecture. He felt in its everyday life a closeness to instinct and passion, which had not survived in the wan and sickened cities of Western Europe. On his return, Rilke tried to keep as much of Russia about him as he could. He launched into a study of Russian literature and went about dressed in Russian peasant garb. When, on September 20, 1899, in Schmargendorf near Berlin, he sat down to write the phrases that spoke themselves within him, it was in the persona of a Russian monk living in a cloister, summoned by the bell to the task of seeing and meeting what was most real to him in the world.

The sixty-seven poems Rilke wrote over the next twenty-five days would form the first part of *The Book of Hours*, called

The Book of a Monastic Life. These intensely inward conversations with God distilled the seeking of the past years for an unmediated and intimate encounter with the heart of the universe. In November he wrote in his journal—the journal in which he never mentioned *The Book of Hours*—"I have begun my life."

It is possible to read *The Book of Hours* as a cycle of love poems, and it is certainly possible to read into their creation the sensuous awakening of Rilke's relationship with Lou. The God of these poems is a God whom Rilke seeks to love and be possessed by with the same passion he has for Lou, and also with the same passion he has for his vocation.

In the summer of 1900, after another and longer Russian sojourn with Lou, Rilke was invited to Worpswede, an artists' colony in the open heath country near Bremen, which was to play a significant role in his life and imagination. Rilke had been urged by Lou toward greater independence from her, and he felt free to develop new relationships. In Worpswede he met Clara Westhoff, a gifted and ardent sculptor three years younger than he. She became pregnant, and they were married on April 28, 1901, at her parents' home, and set up housekeeping in a small cottage in Westerwede. There, as the young couple awaited the birth of their child (a daughter, Ruth, born on December 12), thirty-four poems that were to become the second part of *The Book of Hours*—to be named *The Book of Pilgrimage*—came to Rilke. He wrote them in one week, between September 18 and 25.

As the conversations with God are resumed, *The Book of Pilgrimage* reflects Rilke's acute awareness of humanity's unfolding fate as well as his more personal preoccupations. Images of pregnancy enter the religious discourse: God is described as womb, and more frequently as the new life growing inside the poet.

> *I wish sometimes that you were back inside me,*
> *in this darkness that grew you.*   [II, 4]

Impending fatherhood must have aroused old anger toward the poet's own father. The patriarchal God is rejected now with a vehemence that never occurs in *The Book of a Monastic Life*.

> *His caring is a nightmare to us,*
> *and his voice a stone.*   [II, 6]

Rilke was facing the task of supporting his young family with almost no material resources and no regular employment. His letters that autumn express a pervasive economic anxiety. Usually such insecurity narrows the focus of one's concern; the wonder is that for the poet the opposite happened, and his heart blew open to the suffering of all humanity. Though Rilke reminds God that

> *I'm still the one who knelt before you*
> *in monk's robes,*   [II, 2]

the persona here is more concerned with the world. The pilgrimage on which he finds himself unites him with that world in the depth of his being.

In August 1902, Rilke went to Paris, commissioned to write a monograph on the sculptor Auguste Rodin. He and Clara had decided to change their life and—leaving Ruth predominantly in the care of her maternal grandparents in their comfortable country home—freed each other to pursue their art. Engaged by Rodin as his secretary, Rilke worked long, demanding hours. He was inspired by the sculptor's relentless self-discipline and rededicated himself to the task of poetry with an enhanced respect for craft. But between the demands the great sculptor made on him and his own intense distress over the urban poverty and suffering he beheld in the city around him, Rilke was rarely able to find time or courage for his own work.

In late March 1903, Rilke boarded a train, traveled through the Alpine tunnels to Italy, and took a room at a gardened *pensione* by the sea in Viareggio, which he had loved on his earlier trip. As he wrote to Franz Kappus, to whom the *Letters to a Young Poet* were addressed, he was there to recover from a great physical and moral lassitude. And there, between April 13 and 20, he composed the poems—again thirty-four of them—that make up *The Book of Poverty and Death*, the third in *The Book of Hours*.

Here both death and poverty, viewed so negatively by modern society as evils to flee, are upheld as sources of value and revelation. Instead of canceling life, death is its fruit—and an expression of our most intimate and unique strivings for meaning. This affirmation is all the more poignant in that Rilke had just been warned—by the person he trusted most—of his alleged suicidal tendencies. Apparently he did not resent Lou for making this gratuitous diagnosis at the time of his marriage to Clara, nor was he undone by it; instead he turned death itself into a long-term ally to accompany his life.

The horrors of urban poverty had confronted Rilke in Paris, as he described to Lou in July 1903:

One goes through smells as through many sad rooms. . . .
And what people I met . . . almost every day: fragments of
caryatids on whom the whole pain still lay, the entire structure
of pain, under which they were living, slow as tortoises . . .
and under the foot of each day that trod on them, they were
enduring like tough beetles . . . twitching like bits of a big
chopped-up fish that is already rotting but still alive. . . . Oh
what kind of a world is that! Pieces, pieces of people, parts of
animals, leftovers of things that have been, and everything
still agitated, as though driven about helter-skelter in an eerie
wind, carried and carrying, falling and overtaking each other
as they fall.

The poems about poverty in the third book reflect Rilke's
anguish in Paris, and are chillingly close to the life in cities to-
day. Rilke has been criticized for sentimentalizing poverty—

Look at them standing about—
like wildflowers, which have nowhere else to grow   [III, 19]

yet mainly he was simply trying to take it in, that people can
make one another suffer so. He tried to look at the destitute
with the same tender attention that he would give to a tree. Rilke
was not writing deliberately to effect social change, as was Émile
Zola, for instance; he was doing what from the dictates of his
own spiritual integrity was necessary for any social transfor-
mation. That is the assertion of our essential interconnected-
ness with each other and with everything that lives. This is not
a political tenet as much as a profound experience in the core
of one's being. In that sense these poems arise from the same

mystical oneness (we can call it the body of Christ, Anima Mundi, Buddha nature) that pervaded the two earlier books.

The Publication of
The Book of Hours

What induced Rilke to submit these poems for publication? For one thing, his economic situation remained a source of torment. He could neither support his wife and child on his literary earnings nor abandon his calling as a poet.

In 1904 the Insel Verlag, which had published Rilke's prose work *Tales of God*, secured his promise to deliver another book. But Rilke's production in the year that followed did not prove sufficient for a new collection. So he contemplated the publication of something already written—the *Gebete*—and he received the handwritten manuscript back from Lou. As writers of a century later, we shudder at the thought of there being but a single copy of these poems. How easily Lou could have lost or misplaced it when she changed her residence! In the end, on April 13, 1905, Rilke wrote to the Insel Verlag, recalling his promise to submit a new work and letting them know he had something ready: "a long extensively rounded cycle of poems which encompasses all the progress I have made . . ."

Once that decision was taken, things began to move for Rilke. The book he planned about the sculptor Rodin took Rilke back to Paris and inspired fresh enthusiasm for the creative process. Lectures about Rodin in Dresden and Prague brought him stimulus and attention as well as income. Best of all, he persuaded Lou, for the first time in years, to let him

come to her. To touch again this single most important rela-
tion of his life promised such fulfillment that the whole year
appeared to him as "full of goodness, now it is really to bring
this one event."

The days with Lou met all his expectations. Her presence, and
even walking alone in the woods behind her house, brought
Rilke home to himself. "We often wish you were with us,"
he wrote to his wife, Clara, "as we sit in the garden and read
or talk . . . It is so much more beautiful than I could have
dreamed, because the need was greater than I thought."

Das Stunden-Buch appeared in December in a first printing of
five hundred copies. Rilke had helped the Insel Verlag to choose
the cover: an old Venetian print of a fountain with three jets of
water representing the three books of the cycle. With his share
of the proceeds, Rilke himself acquired a good number of
copies to give to friends. One of the best returns was a review
by the writer and art-lover Karl von der Heyd, who stated that
this work placed Rilke "on the heights of German lyric poetry."

Rilke's Later Life and Work and Its
Relationship to *The Book of Hours*

Even before *The Book of Poverty and Death*, Rilke had begun writ-
ing the poems that would be included in *The Book of Images*, in
a voice more secular and detached than that of *The Book of
Hours*. The poems that followed, collected as *New Poems (Neue
Gedichte)*, cast the focus on the thing observed, away from the
observer's inner experience.

The next two decades of Rilke's development were shaped

by an increasing awareness of his role as artist. This self-consciousness replaced the naked, transparent approach to things that characterizes *The Book of Hours*. The capacity to shed his ever more burdensome self-image as poet was not available to him again until February 1922. Then, in a period of less than a month, taken by a trancelike inspiration much like that which had produced each sequence of *The Book of Hours*, Rilke composed all fifty-nine *Sonnets to Orpheus* and completed the *Duino Elegies*, begun ten years earlier.

Rilke's life throughout those intervening years 1903 to 1922 had been a pilgrimage in the service of his art. They had been difficult years of struggle for material survival, restless years of repeated moves from one place to another. Rilke was bedeviled by his dependence on the generosity of benefactors, yet he could not give himself to any work save writing. "It is my old inadequacy," he wrote to Clara. "I have only a single energy which cannot be dispersed." These were years, too, of repeated liaisons, intense involvements that shattered ever again on the rocks of his necessary solitude. Each time Rilke fell in love, he confronted his fear of being sidetracked and consumed. Although he maintained a voluminous correspondence, he lived by himself, refusing even the companionship of animals.

As the years went on, his search for the sacred was supplanted by a tendency to see in everything he encountered "a challenge, a task, a claim to artistic transformation." It is not that Rilke lost his hunger for God; rather, it became transmuted into a single-pointed dedication to art that absorbed into itself everything else in his life. Never again, after *The Book of Hours*, would the dynamic between God and the world be expressed in such immediate and reciprocal terms.

In 1912, ill and depressed and moored in a spell of aridity, Rilke was staying alone at Duino Castle near Trieste, the guest of Princess Maria von Thurn und Taxis. There, one morning, the first lines of the *Duino Elegies* came to him—by divine inspiration, as he later told the princess. Within weeks he had completed the first two elegies; but after that, although he knew there was more to come, Rilke was unable to write the rest. He wandered, frustrated, agitated, in search of circumstances hospitable to his work. In a Europe gearing up for the First World War, Rilke's inner turbulence found no place to be assuaged. More travels, more illness, more troubled relationships; a little work on the *Elegies* now and again; a good deal of public acclaim. But inwardly a lack of vitality plagued Rilke, and despair over the violence and nationalism ravaging his world. In December 1917, he wrote in response to a letter from an admirer of *The Book of Hours*: "I'm not living my own life. . . . I feel refuted, abandoned, and above all threatened by a world ready to dissolve entire in such senseless disorder."

When he was at last able to pick up the thread of the *Elegies*, the spirit from which he wrote was deeply reminiscent of the one that had produced *The Book of Hours*. As he was to write in 1925 to Witold von Hulewicz, his Polish translator, Rilke regarded the *Elegies* as "a further shaping of those essential [inspirations] which had been given already in *The Book of Hours*."

Rilke never repudiated *The Book of Hours*. He maintained that a substantial continuity existed between it and all subsequent works. What had changed most between the inspiration of 1899 and that of 1922 was the almost exclusive stress he put on the function of poetry itself. In the old dialectic equation between person and God, the role of the human became emphasized to the point of isolation—

> *If I cried out, who*
> *in the hierarchies of angels*
> *would hear me?*

—and that at a most terrifying juncture of history.

Yet still Rilke knew how to sing, and with a singleness of heart, as if the world depended on it:

> *. . . Could we be here, then,*
> *in order to say: house,*
> *bridge, fountain, gate, pitcher, apple-tree, window . . .*
>
> *And the things, even as they pass,*
> *understand that we praise them.*
> *Transient, they are trusting us*
> *to save them—us, the most transient of all.*

As he wrote these lines of the beloved ninth *Duino Elegy*, the younger Rilke must have taken hold—the one who in 1899 had told God:

> *. . . I want to portray you*
> *not with lapis or gold, but with colors made of apple bark. . . .*
> *I want, then, simply*
> *to say the names of things.*   [I, 60]

and:

> I would describe myself
> like a landscape I've studied
> at length, in detail;
> like a word I'm coming to understand;
> like a pitcher I pour from at mealtime;
> like my mother's face;
> like a ship that carried me
> when the waters raged.   [I, 13]

Rilke never lost his conviction in the utter reality of the world, or in our human capacity to redeem it through that act of transforming attention, which is naming—or love.

The Growing Relevance of These Poems

As we prepare this centenary publication, we are struck by the extent to which the poems of *The Book of Hours* seem even more relevant to our moment in history than when we first brought out our translations in 1996. In the nine years that have elapsed since then, swift and profound changes have overtaken our society, generating widespread anguish and uncertainty. These poems reveal ever richer meaning as they speak to this troubled spirit. Many of the poems, reread today, seem predictive of the disastrous developments we now face and the signs of an approaching end that we are bringing about.

When the poet greets the new (twentieth) century, it is with foreboding:

I'm living just as the century ends . . .
We see the brightness of a new page
Where everything yet can happen.

Unmoved by us, the fates take its measure
and look at one another, saying nothing.   [I, 8]

After evoking the many life-affirming ways in which we experience the divine, the poet pauses and simply invites God to let go:

Let your hand rest on the rim of heaven now
and mutely bear the darkness we bring over you.   [I, 25]

The poet is unafraid to name the final loss. The very naming strengthens the soul—as does the call to not allow that loss to diminish our love.

Dear darkening ground,
you've endured so patiently the walls we've built,
perhaps you'll give the cities one more hour . . .

before you become forest again, and water, and widening
      wilderness
in that hour of inconceivable terror
when you take back your name from all things.

Just give me a little more time!
I want to love the things
As no one has thought to love them,
Until they're worthy of you and real. [I, 61]

The destructive forces we face are not external or accidental, but endemic to the very foundations of our society. The poet sees the intrinsic brutality of a culture driven by greed:

The kings of the world are old and feeble . . .
Their sons are dying before they are men,
and their pale daughters
abandon themselves to the brokers of violence.

Their crowns are exchanged for money
and melted down into machines . . . [II, 24]

Lord, the great cities are lost and rotting . . . [III, 4–5]

We humans are not exempt from this decay; we are contaminated, both physically and morally:

In alleyways I sweep myself up
out of garbage and broken glass . . .
I am a city by the sea
sinking into a toxic tide.
I am strange to myself, as though someone unknown
had poisoned my mother as she carried me. [II, 2]

Rilke's capacity to face this utter degradation reveals his acuteness of perception and his courage. The lyric romantic tradition, which shaped him as a poet, did not blur his vision nor blunt his moral indictment. The raw realism with which he saw and portrayed urban poverty is yet more telling today than it was a mere decade ago.

For those of us who cannot take comfort in an absolute and triumphalist God, immune to suffering, the God of *The Book of Hours* is more appealing than ever. These poems speak to our tacit knowledge that only in confronting our shame can we redeem our lives. This redemption is not mediated by any priest, preacher, or institution, but is inseparable from the living body of Earth.

> *. . . Whom should I turn to,*
> *if not the one whose darkness*
> *is darker than night, the only one*
> *who keeps vigil with no candle,*
> *and is not afraid—*
> *the deep one, whose being I trust,*
> *for it breaks through the earth into trees,*
> *and rises,*
> *when I bow my head,*
> *faint as a fragrance*
> *from the soil.* [II, 3]

Notes on the Translation

In submitting ourselves to these poems over a period of twelve years, each of us has been deeply nourished by them. Thus, in successive revisions, we have been able to make changes in part effected by the changes the poems themselves have effected in us. As we reviewed this book for the new, centenary edition, we added four more poems and made changes in our translation of a number of the others. In doing so, we were struck again by the way these poems continue to yield fresh meanings and even greater relevance to our time.

Translation, as George Steiner points out, is, among other things, a work of self-denial, demanding that the translator serve the original rather than impose herself on it. However, as Steiner also points out, all translation—like all reading and even all listening—is a work of editing, a work of interpretation, determined by subjective and contextual factors.

Because our translation differs significantly from other translations of these poems, we will point out the kinds of decisions we made concerning form, sound, and substance.

Rilke wrote the poems of *The Book of Hours* in rhymed, metered verse. In many cases the rhyme scheme was ABAB and the rhythm iambic quatrameter, forms that today sound too singsong to convey the seriousness of Rilke's meaning. In addition, the opening of form in American poetry, particularly since the beginning of the twentieth century, reflects the uncertainty and ambiguities of this modern age.

The question, then, of how to be faithful to the musicality of Rilke's poetry without imitating his technique has challenged us through the course of our work. We have chosen to adopt certain of his technical devices—alliteration, the repetition of certain sounds and internal rhymes, for instance—in order to give the reader without German some intimation of the beauty of the original. Here are some examples to show how we worked. We believe that the sound achieved here is a result of our working aloud together.

At some points, in order to lend the English some echo of the rhyme in the original, we chose assonance over outright duplication of the sound—a standard device known as slant rhyme.

Dich wundert nicht des Sturmes Wucht
du hast ihn wachsen sehn:
die Bäume fluchten. Ihre flucht
schafft schreitende Alleen. [II, 1]

You are not surprised at the force of the storm—
you have seen it growing.
The trees flee. Their flight
sets the boulevards streaming.

Another example:

Ich bin dein Krug (wenn ich zerscherbe?)
Ich bin dein Trank (wenn ich verderbe?)   [I, 36]

I am your pitcher (when I shatter?)
I am your drink (when I go bitter?)

We also, in some cases, achieved an internal rhyme resonant with Rilke's:

Nirgends will ich gebogen bleiben,
denn dort bin ich gelogen, wo ich gebogen bin.
                              [I, 13]

we translated:

I want to unfold.
Let no place in me hold itself closed,
for where I am closed, I am false.

Rilke makes ample use of alliteration, which, at times, we were able to render directly into English, given the similarities between the languages.

> *Und ich seh dich in meinen Gesichten mit Winden,*
> *Wassern, und Wäldern*
> *rauschend am Rande des Christentums* [I, 60]

becomes:

> *But now I see you:*
> *wind, woods, and water,*
> *roaring at the rim of Christendom.*

Or:

> *Ihr vielen unbestürmten Städte* [I, 49]

is rendered as:

> *You many unassaulted cities.*

In instances where the rhythm of the original felt appropriate to render in English, we did so. For example, the strong first syllables of I, 19,

> *Ich bin, du Angstlicher,*

we translated:

> *I am, you anxious one,*

which scans precisely as the German. In other instances, such as II, 25,

Alles wird wieder gross sein und gewaltig,

while we could not imitate the rhythm of the original, we wanted to match the rather exuberant major key of the German (which marks a shift in tone from the poems preceding it) with a rhythm in English auspicious enough to make the shift evident. Thus we chose the heavy, drumlike beat,

All will come again into its strength.

We sought always to retain the luminous simplicity Rilke achieved in these poems, while staying faithful to his subtlety of thought. This led at times to our choosing an English word that, although not literally present in the German, conveyed more precisely the spirit of the original.

Ich bin die Welt,
aus der er irrend fiel [1, 35]

would translate literally: "I am the world out of which he, erring, fell." We translated this at first: "I am the world that he fell out of." But on revision we realized that "fell" carried the connotation of Lucifer's fall, and not the sense of mistakenness. Another verb occurred to us, and thus, "I am the world / he stumbled out of," as a way of holding both meanings, fall and error, and of retaining the brevity of the original.

In a similar vein, we chose at times to be faithful to the metaphoric, rather than the literal, meaning of the text, where the literal in English was clumsy or even absurd. In I, 59, for instance, God says, *"Gib mir Gewand,"* literally "Give me clothing." We translated this, "Embody me," to convey the task we are to perform for God in the world. In I, 3,

> *Doch wie ich mich auch in mich selber neige:*
> *Mein Gott ist dunkel und wie em Gewebe*

is literally:

> *Yet as I also lean into myself:*
> *My God is dark and like a web.*

We translated:

> *But when I lean over the chasm of myself*
> *it seems*
> *my God is dark*
> *and like a web.*

"Chasm," an image invoked several times in *The Book of Hours*, conveys the contrast Rilke makes in this poem between himself and his more confident and conventional brother-monks. J. B. Leishman's translation of this line is: "How, though, into myself I keep inclining!" (Leishman's exclamation point).

The above lines indicate the liberties we sometimes took with spacing. In contrast to much American poetry of the past few decades, *The Book of Hours* relies mostly on end-stopped lines, which break at more or less obvious units of thought. Translating for our own time, we often changed the more classic line breaks in order to reflect the open and groping nature of Rilke's thought. Frequently, however, as we reworked the poems, we broke the lines in a manner more consistent with the original.

A major decision, of course, involved which poems and which parts of poems to translate. Of the one hundred thirty-five poems of *Das Stundenbuch* we have translated eighty-four. We omitted some lines and even entire sections of poems, and collapsed two consecutive poems into one. We have noted such changes in our commentary.

These poems were translated in our homes in the San Francisco Bay area and on several brief retreats in Inverness and Philo, California. Some of them were translated in bright sunshine overlooking Tomales Bay (from suite 11 at the Golden Hinde). Most were translated indoors, between teaching engagements across the U.S. and overseas. They were translated during ongoing crises in our world, with survival of life on our planet increasingly endangered. Our work together on these poems brought a measure of stillness and reflection. Like an underground river, it related to and nourished all the rest.

From the start, we had a distinctive way of working. We translated aloud, reading and rereading the German, talking about it, then suggesting English wording to each other. Because of this, it is impossible to attribute any aspect of any of the poems to one or the other of us. The effort—including the commentary, the introduction, and these notes—has been wholly collaborative. The fact that there were two of us allowed a level of comprehension to emerge that might have eluded either of us alone. This dialogic process helped keep us faithful to the spirit of the original. Every decision was mutual.

Most of all we are thankful for the young man who, standing at the cusp of the last century, with all that it would bring to pass, opened the treasure house of his mind and heart. We, who stand at the beginning of this one, bow to him in deep acknowledgment. It is a great blessing to live with these poems and to offer them to others.

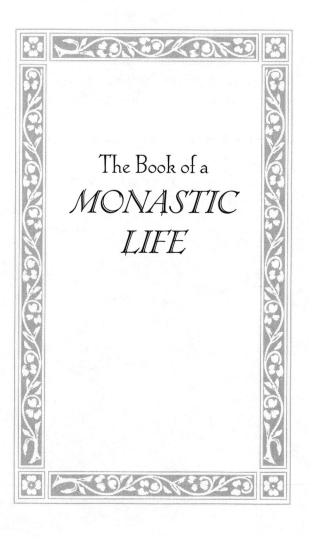

The Book of a
*MONASTIC
LIFE*

Da neigt sich die Stunde und rührt mich an
mit klarem, metallenem Schlag:
mir zittern die Sinne. Ich fühle: ich kann—
und ich fasse den plastischen Tag.

Nichts war noch vollendet, eh ich es erschaut,
ein jedes Werden stand still.
Meine Blicke sind reif, und wie eine Braut
kommt jedem das Ding, das er will . . .

I, 1

The hour is striking so close above me,
so clear and sharp,
that all my senses ring with it.
I feel it now: there's a power in me
to grasp and give shape to my world.

I know that nothing has ever been real
without my beholding it.
All becoming has needed me.
My looking ripens things
and they come toward me, to meet and be met.

I, 1

Ich lebe mein Leben in wachsenden Ringen,
die sich über die Dinge ziehn.
Ich werde den letzten vielleicht nicht vollbringen,
aber versuchen will ich ihn.

Ich kreise um Gott, um den uralten Turm,
und ich kreise jahrtausendelang;
und ich weiß noch nicht: bin ich ein Falke, ein Sturm
oder ein großer Gesang.

I, 2

I live my life in widening circles
that reach out across the world.
I may not complete this last one
but I give myself to it.

I circle around God, around the primordial tower.
I've been circling for thousands of years
and I still don't know: am I a falcon,
a storm, or a great song?

I, 2

Ich habe viele Brüder in Sutanen
im Süden, wo in Klöstern Lorbeer steht.
Ich weiß, wie menschlich sie Madonnen planen,
und träume oft von jungen Tizianen,
durch die der Gott in Gluten geht.

Doch wie ich mich auch in mich selber neige:
Mein Gott ist dunkel und wie ein Gewebe
von hundert Wurzeln, welche schweigsam trinken.
Nur, daß ich mich aus seiner Wärme hebe,
mehr weiß ich nicht, weil alle meine Zweige
tief unten ruhn und nur im Winde winken.

I, 3

I have many brothers in the South
who move, handsome in their vestments,
through cloister gardens.
The Madonnas they make are so human,
and I dream often of their Titians,
where God becomes an ardent flame.

But when I lean over the chasm of myself—
it seems
my God is dark
and like a web: a hundred roots
silently drinking.

This is the ferment I grow out of.

More I don't know, because my branches
rest in deep silence, stirred only by the wind.

I, 3

Wir dürfen dich nicht eigenmächtig malen,
du Dämmernde, aus der der Morgen stieg.
Wir holen aus den alten Farbenschalen
die gleichen Striche und die gleichen Strahlen,
mit denen dich der Heilige verschwieg.

Wir bauen Bilder vor dir auf wie Wände;
so daß schon tausend Mauern um dich stehn.
Denn dich verhüllen unsre frommen Hände,
sooft dich unsre Herzen offen sehn.

I, 4

We must not portray you in king's robes,
you drifting mist that brought forth the morning.

Once again from the old paintboxes
we take the same gold for scepter and crown
that has disguised you through the ages.

Piously we produce our images of you
till they stand around you like a thousand walls.
And when our hearts would simply open,
our fervent hands hide you.

I, 4

Ich liebe meines Wesens Dunkelstunden,
in welchen meine Sinne sich vertiefen;
in ihnen hab ich, wie in alten Briefen,
mein täglich Leben schon gelebt gefunden
und wie Legende weit und überwunden.

Aus ihnen kommt mir Wissen, daß ich Raum
zu einem zweiten zeitlos breiten Leben habe.

Und manchmal bin ich wie der Baum,
der, reif und rauschend, über einem Grabe
den Traum erfüllt, den der vergangne Knabe
(um den sich seine warmen Wurzeln drängen)
verlor in Traurigkeiten und Gesängen.

I, 5

I love the dark hours of my being.
My mind deepens into them.
There I can find, as in old letters,
the days of my life, already lived,
and held like a legend, and understood.

Then the knowing comes: I can open
to another life that's wide and timeless.

So I am sometimes like a tree
rustling over a gravesite
and making real the dream
of the one its living roots
embrace:

a dream once lost
among sorrows and songs.

I, 5

Du, Nachbar Gott, wenn ich dich manchesmal
in langer Nacht mit hartem Klopfen störe,—
so ists, weil ich dich selten atmen höre
und weiß: Du bist allein im Saal.
Und wenn du etwas brauchst, ist keiner da,
um deinem Tasten einen Trank zu reichen:
Ich horche immer. Gieb ein kleines Zeichen.
Ich bin ganz nah.

Nur eine schmale Wand ist zwischen uns,
durch Zufall; denn es könnte sein:
ein Rufen deines oder meines Munds—
und sie bricht ein
ganz ohne Lärm und Laut . . .

I, 6

You, God, who live next door—

If at times, through the long night, I trouble you
with my urgent knocking—
this is why: I hear you breathe so seldom.
I know you're all alone in that room.
If you should be thirsty, there's no one
to get you a glass of water.
I wait listening, always. Just give me a sign!
I'm right here.

As it happens, the wall between us
is very thin. Why couldn't a cry
from one of us
break it down? It would crumble
easily,

it would barely make a sound.

I, 6

Wenn es nur einmal so ganz stille wäre.
Wenn das Zufällige und Ungefähre
verstummte und das nachbarliche Lachen,
wenn das Geräusch, das meine Sinne machen,
mich nicht so sehr verhinderte am Wachen—:

Dann könnte ich in einem tausendfachen
Gedanken bis an deinen Rand dich denken
und dich besitzen (nur ein Lächeln lang),
um dich an alles Leben zu verschenken
wie einen Dank.

I, 7

If only for once it were still.
If the *not quite right* and the *why this*
could be muted, and the neighbor's laughter,
and the static my senses make—
if all of it didn't keep me from coming awake—

Then in one vast thousandfold thought
I could think you up to where thinking ends.

I could possess you,
even for the brevity of a smile,
to offer you
to all that lives,
in gladness.

I, 7

Ich lebe grad, da das Jahrhundert geht.
Man fühlt den Wind von einem großen Blatt,
das Gott und du und ich beschrieben hat
und das sich hoch in fremden Händen dreht.

Man fühlt den Glanz von einer neuen Seite,
auf der noch Alles werden kann.

Die stillen Kräfte prüfen ihre Breite
und sehn einander dunkel an.

I, 8

I'm living just as the century ends.

A great leaf, that God and you and I
have covered with writing
turns now, overhead, in strange hands.
We feel the sweep of it like a wind.

We see the brightness of a new page
where everything yet can happen.

Unmoved by us, the fates take its measure
and look at one another, saying nothing.

I, 8

Ich lese es heraus aus deinem Wort,
aus der Geschichte der Gebärden,
mit welchen deine Hände um das Werden
sich ründeten, begrenzend, warm und weise.
Du sagtest leben laut und sterben leise
und wiederholtest immer wieder: *Sein*.
Doch vor dem ersten Tode kam der Mord.
Da ging ein Riß durch deine reifen Kreise
und ging ein Schrein
und riß die Stimmen fort,
die eben erst sich sammelten
um dich zu sagen,
um dich zu tragen
alles Abgrunds Brücke—

Und was sie seither stammelten,
sind Stücke
deines alten Namens.

I, 9

I read it here in your very word,
in the story of the gestures
with which your hands cupped themselves
around our becoming—limiting, warm.

You said *live* out loud, and *die* you said lightly,
and over and over again you said *be*.

But before the first death came murder.
A fracture broke across the rings you'd ripened.
A screaming shattered the voices

that had just come together to speak you,
to make of you a bridge
over the chasm of everything.

And what they have stammered ever since
are fragments
of your ancient name.

I, 9

Der blasse Abelknabe spricht:

Ich bin nicht. Der Bruder hat mir was getan,
was meine Augen nicht sahn.
Er hat mir das Licht verhängt.
Er hat mein Gesicht verdrängt
mit seinem Gesicht.
Er ist jetzt allein.
Ich denke, er muß noch sein.
Denn ihm tut niemand, wie er mir getan.
Es gingen alle meine Bahn,
kommen alle vor seinen Zorn,
gehen alle an ihm verloren.

Ich glaube, mein großer Bruder wacht
wie ein Gericht.
An mich hat die Nacht gedacht;
an ihn nicht.

I, 10

(Abel speaks)

I am not. The brother did something to me
that my eyes didn't see.
He veiled the light.
He hid my face with his face.
Now he is alone.
I think he must still exist,
for no one does to him what he did to me.
All have gone the same way:
all are met with his rage,
beside him all are lost.

I sense my older brother lies awake
as if accused.
Night offers itself to me,
not to him.

I, 10

Du Dunkelheit, aus der ich stamme,
ich liebe dich mehr als die Flamme,
welche die Welt begrenzt,
indem sie glänzt
für irgend einen Kreis,
aus dem heraus kein Wesen von ihr weiß.

Aber die Dunkelheit hält alles an sich:
Gestalten und Flammen, Tiere und mich,
wie sie's errafft,
Menschen und Mächte—

Und es kann sein: eine große Kraft
rührt sich in meiner Nachbarschaft.

Ich glaube an Nächte.

I, 11

You, darkness, of whom I am born—

I love you more than the flame
that limits the world
to the circle it illumines
and excludes all the rest.

But the dark embraces everything:
shapes and shadows, creatures and me,
people, nations—just as they are.

It lets me imagine
a great presence stirring beside me.

I believe in the night.

I, 11

Ich glaube an Alles noch nie Gesagte.
Ich will meine frömmsten Gefühle befrein.
Was noch keiner zu wollen wagte,
wird mir einmal unwillkürlich sein.

Ist das vermessen, mein Gott, vergieb.
Aber ich will dir damit nur sagen:
Meine beste Kraft soll sein wie ein Trieb,
so ohne Zürnen und ohne Zagen;
so haben dich ja die Kinder lieb.

Mit diesem Hinfluten, mit diesem Münden
in breiten Armen ins offene Meer,
mit dieser wachsenden Wiederkehr
will ich dich bekennen, will ich dich verkünden
wie keiner vorher . . .

I, 12

I believe in all that has never yet been spoken.
I want to free what waits within me
so that what no one has dared to wish for
may for once spring clear
without my contriving.

If this is arrogant, God, forgive me,
but this is what I need to say.
May what I do flow from me like a river,
no forcing and no holding back,
the way it is with children.

Then in these swelling and ebbing currents,
these deepening tides moving out, returning,
I will sing you as no one ever has,
streaming through widening channels
into the open sea.

I, 12

Ich bin auf der Welt zu allein und doch nicht allein
        genug
um jede Stunde zu weihn.
Ich bin auf der Welt zu gering und doch nicht klein genug
um vor dir zu sein wie ein Ding,
dunkel und klug.
Ich will meinen Willen und will meinen Willen begleiten
die Wege zur Tat;
und will in stillen, irgendwie zögernden Zeiten,
wenn etwas naht,
unter den Wissenden sein
oder allein.

Ich will dich immer spiegeln in ganzer Gestalt,
und will niemals blind sein oder zu alt
um dein schweres schwankendes Bild zu halten.
Ich will mich entfalten.
Nirgends will ich gebogen bleiben,
denn dort bin ich gelogen, wo ich gebogen bin.
Und ich will meinen Sinn
wahr vor dir. Ich will mich beschreiben
wie ein Bild das ich sah,
lange und nah,
wie ein Wort, das ich begriff,

I'm too alone in the world, yet not alone enough
to make each hour holy.
I'm too small in the world, yet not small enough
to be simply in your presence, like a thing—
just as it is.

I want to know my own will
and to move with it.
And I want, in the hushed moments
when the nameless draws near,
to be among the wise ones—
or alone.

I want to mirror your immensity.
I want never to be too weak or too old
to bear the heavy, lurching image of you.

I want to unfold.
Let no place in me hold itself closed,
for where I am closed, I am false.
I want to stay clear in your sight.

wie meinen täglichen Krug,
wie meiner Mutter Gesicht,
wie ein Schiff,
das mich trug
durch den tödlichsten Sturm.

I, 13

I would describe myself
like a landscape I've studied
at length, in detail;
like a word I'm coming to understand;
like a pitcher I pour from at mealtime;
like my mother's face;
like a ship that carried me
when the waters raged.

I, 13

Du siehst, ich will viel.
Vielleicht will ich Alles:
das Dunkel jedes unendlichen Falles
und jedes Steigens lichtzitterndes Spiel.

Es leben so viele und wollen nichts,
und sind durch ihres leichten Gerichts
glatte Gefühle gefürstet.

Aber du freust dich jedes Gesichts,
das dient und dürstet.

Du freust dich Aller, die dich gebrauchen
wie ein Gerät.

Noch bist du nicht kalt, und es ist nicht zu spät,
in deine werdenden Tiefen zu tauchen,
wo sich das Leben ruhig verrät.

I, 14

You see, I want a lot.
Maybe I want it all:
the darkness of each endless fall,
the shimmering light of each ascent.

So many are alive who don't seem to care.
Casual, easy, they move in the world
as though untouched.

But you take pleasure in the faces
of those who know they thirst.
You cherish those
who grip you for survival.

You are not dead yet, it's not too late
to open your depths by plunging into them
and drink in the life
that reveals itself quietly there.

I, 14

Wir bauen an dir mit zitternden Händen
und wir türmen Atom auf Atom.
Aber wer kann dich vollenden,
du Dom.

Was ist Rom?
Es zerfällt.
Was ist die Welt?
Sie wird zerschlagen
eh deine Türme Kuppeln tragen,
eh aus Meilen von Mosaik
deine strahlende Stirne stieg.

Aber manchmal im Traum
kann ich deinen Raum
überschaun,
tief vom Beginne
bis zu des Daches goldenem Grate.

Und ich seh: meine Sinne
bilden und baun
die letzten Zierate.

I, 15

Our hands shake as we try to construct you,
block on block.
But you, cathedral we dimly perceive—
who can bring you to completion?

What's Rome? It crumbled.
What is the world? We are destroying it
before your towers can taper into spires,
before we can assemble your face
from the piles of mosaic.

Yet sometimes in dreams
I take in your whole expanse,
from its deepest beginnings
up to the rooftop's glittering ridge.

And then I see: it is my mind
that will fashion
and set the last pieces in place.

I, 15

Daraus, daß Einer dich einmal gewollt hat,
weiß ich, daß wir dich wollen dürfen.
Wenn wir auch alle Tiefen verwürfen:
wenn ein Gebirge Gold hat
und keiner mehr es ergraben mag,
trägt es einmal der Fluß zutag,
der in die Stille der Steine greift,
der vollen.

Auch wenn wir nicht wollen:
Gott reift.

I, 16

Because once someone dared
to want you,
I know that we, too, may want you.

When gold is in the mountain
and we've ravaged the depths
till we've given up digging,

it will be brought forth into day
by the river that mines
the silences of stone.

Even when we don't desire it,
God is ripening.

I, 16

Wer seines Lebens viele Widersinne
versöhnt und dankbar in ein Sinnbild faßt,
der drängt
die Lärmenden aus dem Palast,
wird *anders* festlich, und du bist der Gast,
den er an sanften Abenden empfängt.

Du bist der Zweite seiner Einsamkeit,
die ruhige Mitte seinen Monologen;
und jeder Kreis, um dich gezogen,
spannt ihm den Zirkel aus der Zeit.

I, 17

She who reconciles the ill-matched threads
of her life, and weaves them gratefully
into a single cloth—
it's she who drives the loudmouths from the hall
and clears it for a different celebration

where the one guest is you.
In the softness of evening
it's you she receives.

You are the partner of her loneliness,
the unspeaking center of her monologues.
With each disclosure you encompass more
and she stretches beyond what limits her,
to hold you.

I, 17

Was irren meine Hände in den Pinseln?
Wenn ich dich *male*, Gott, du merkst es kaum.

Ich *fühle* dich. An meiner Sinne Saum
beginnst du zögernd, wie mit vielen Inseln,
und deinen Augen, welche niemals blinseln,
bin ich der Raum.

Du bist nicht mehr inmitten deines Glanzes,
wo alle Linien des Engeltanzes
die Fernen dir verbrauchen wie Musik,—
du wohnst in deinem allerletzten Haus.
Dein ganzer Himmel horcht in mich hinaus,
weil ich mich sinnend dir verschwieg.

I, 18

Why am I reaching again for the brushes?
When I paint your portrait, God,
nothing happens.

But I can choose to feel you.

At my senses' horizon
you appear hesitantly,
like scattered islands.

Yet standing here, peering out,
I'm all the time seen by you.

The choruses of angels use up all of heaven.
There's no more room for you
in all that glory. You're living
in your very last house.

All creation holds its breath, listening within me,
because, to hear you, I keep silent.

I, 18

Ich bin, du Ängstlicher. Hörst du mich nicht
mit allen meinen Sinnen an dir branden?
Meine Gefühle, welche Flügel fanden,
umkreisen weiß dein Angesicht.
Siehst du nicht meine Seele, wie sie dicht
vor dir in einem Kleid aus Stille steht?
Reift nicht mein mailiches Gebet
an deinem Blicke wie an einem Baum?

Wenn du der Träumer bist, bin ich dein Traum.
Doch wenn du wachen willst, bin ich dein Wille
und werde mächtig aller Herrlichkeit
und ründe mich wie eine Sternenstille
über der wunderlichen Stadt der Zeit.

I, 19

I am, you anxious one.

Don't you sense me, ready to break
into being at your touch?
My murmurings surround you like shadowy wings.
Can't you see me standing before you
cloaked in stillness?
Hasn't my longing ripened in you
from the beginning
as fruit ripens on a branch?

I am the dream you are dreaming.
When you want to awaken, I am that wanting:
I grow strong in the beauty you behold.
And with the silence of stars I enfold
your cities made by time.

I, 19

Wenn ich gewachsen wäre irgendwo,
wo leichtere Tage sind und schlanke Stunden,
ich hätte dir ein großes Fest erfunden,
und meine Hände hielten dich nicht so,
wie sie dich manchmal halten, bang und hart.

Dort hätte ich gewagt, dich zu vergeuden,
du grenzenlose Gegenwart.
Wie einen Ball
hätt ich dich in alle wogenden Freuden
hineingeschleudert, daß einer dich finge
und deinem Fall
mit hohen Händen entgegenspringe,
du Ding der Dinge . . .

Gemalt hätt ich dich: nicht an die Wand,
an den Himmel selber von Rand zu Rand,
und hätt dich gebildet, wie ein Gigant
dich bilden würde: als Berg, als Brand,
als Samum, wachsend aus Wüstensand . . .

I, 21

If I had grown in some generous place—
if my hours had opened in ease—
I would make you a lavish banquet.
My hands wouldn't clutch at you like this,
so needy and tight.

Then I'd have dared to squander you,
you Limitless Now.
I'd have tossed you into the ringing air
like a ball that someone leaps for and catches
with hands outstretched.

I would have painted you: not on the wall
but in one broad sweep across heaven.
I'd have portrayed you brashly:

as mountain, as fire, as a wind
howling from the desert's vastness.

I, 21

Ich finde dich in allen diesen Dingen,
denen ich gut und wie ein Bruder bin;
als Samen sonnst du dich in den geringen
und in den großen giebst du groß dich hin.

Das ist das wundersame Spiel der Kräfte,
daß sie so dienend durch die Dinge gehn:
in Wurzeln wachsend, schwindend in die Schäfte
und in den Wipfeln wie ein Auferstehn.

I, 22

I find you there in all these things
I care for like a brother.
A seed, you nestle in the smallest of them,
and in the huge ones spread yourself hugely.

Such is the amazing play of the powers:
they give themselves so willingly,
swelling in the roots, thinning as the trunks rise,
and in the high leaves, resurrection.

I, 22

Stimme eines jungen Bruders

Ich verrinne, ich verrinne
wie Sand, der durch Finger rinnt.
Ich habe auf einmal so viele Sinne,
die alle anders durstig sind.
Ich fühle mich an hundert Stellen
schwellen und schmerzen.
Aber am meisten mitten im Herzen.

Ich möchte sterben. Laß mich allein.
Ich glaube, es wird mir gelingen,
so bange zu sein,
daß mir die Pulse zerspringen.

I, 23

(Voice of a younger brother)

I'm slipping, I'm slipping away
like sand

slipping through fingers. All
my cells

are open, and all
so thirsty. I ache and swell

in a hundred places, but mostly
in the middle of my heart.

I want to die. Leave me alone.
I feel I am almost there—

where the great terror
can dismember me.

I, 23

Ich liebe dich, du sanftestes Gesetz,
an dem wir reiften, da wir mit ihm rangen;
du großes Heimweh, das wir nicht bezwangen,
du Wald, aus dem wir nie hinausgegangen,
du Lied, das wir mit jedem Schweigen sangen,
du dunkles Netz,
darin sich flüchtend die Gefühle fangen.

Du hast dich so unendlich groß begonnen
an jenem Tage, da du uns begannst,—
und wir sind so gereift in deinen Sonnen,
so breit geworden und so tief gepflanzt,
daß du in Menschen, Engeln und Madonnen
dich ruhend jetzt vollenden kannst.

Laß deine Hand am Hang der Himmel ruhn
und dulde stumm, was wir dir dunkel tun.

I, 25

I love you, gentlest of Ways,
who ripened us as we wrestled with you.

You, the great homesickness we could never shake off,
you, the forest that always surrounded us,

you, the song we sang in every silence,
you dark net threading through us,

You began yourself so greatly
on that day when you began us—
and we have so ripened in your sunlight,
spreading far and firmly planted—
that now in all people, angels, madonnas,
you can decide: the work is done.

Let your hand rest on the rim of Heaven now
and mutely bear the darkness we bring over you.

I, 25

Das waren Tage Michelangelo's,
von denen ich in fremden Büchern las.
Das war der Mann, der über einem Maß,
gigantengroß,
die Unermeßlichkeit vergaß.

Das war der Mann, der immer wiederkehrt,
wenn eine Zeit noch einmal ihren Wert,
da sie sich enden will, zusammenfaßt.
Da hebt noch einer ihre ganze Last
und wirft sie in den Abgrund seiner Brust.

Die vor ihm hatten Leid und Lust;
er aber fühlt nur noch des Lebens Masse
und daß er Alles wie *ein* Ding umfasse, —
nur Gott bleibt über seinem Willen weit:
da liebt er ihn mit seinem hohen Hasse
für diese Unerreichbarkeit.

I, 29

Once I read in foreign books
of the time of Michelangelo.
That was a man beyond measure—a giant—
who forgot what the immeasurable was.

He was the kind of man who turns
to bring forth the meaning of an age
that wants to end.
He lifts its whole weight
and heaves it into the chasm of his heart.

The anguish and yearning of all those before him
become in his hands raw matter
for him to compress into one great work.

Only God escapes his will—a God
he loves with a high hatred
for being so out of reach.

I, 29

Ich kann nicht glauben, daß der kleine Tod,
dem wir doch täglich übern Scheitel schauen,
uns eine Sorge bleibt und eine Not.

Ich kann nicht glauben, daß er ernsthaft droht;
ich lebe noch, ich habe Zeit zu bauen:
mein Blut ist länger als die Rosen rot.

Mein Sinn ist tiefer als das witzige Spiel
mit unsrer Furcht, darin er sich gefällt.
Ich bin die Welt,
aus der er irrend fiel.

                              Wie er
kreisende Mönche wandern so umher;
man fürchtet sich vor ihrer Wiederkehr,
man weiß nicht: ist es jedesmal derselbe,
sinds zwei, sinds zehn, sinds tausend oder mehr?
Man kennt nur diese fremde gelbe Hand,
die sich ausstreckt so nackt und nah—
da da:
als käm sie aus dem eigenen Gewand.

                                        I, 35

I cannot believe that little death
whom we busily ignore
remains for us a sorrow and a need.

I cannot believe he is that menacing.
I'm still alive, I have time to build.
My blood will outlast the rose.

My knowing is deeper than the teasing way
he likes to toy with our fear.
I am the world
he stumbled out of.

Yet each time the slow procession passes
we're afraid to look.
We don't know: is it the same
as before? is it two now? or ten?
or a thousand? more?

We only know
the cold waxen hand
so naked and near
could be our own.

I, 35

Was wirst du tun, Gott, wenn ich sterbe?
Ich bin dein Krug (wenn ich zerscherbe?)
Ich bin dein Trank (wenn ich verderbe?)
Bin dein Gewand und dein Gewerbe,
mit mir verlierst du deinen Sinn.

Nach mir hast du kein Haus, darin
dich Worte, nah und warm, begrüßen.
Es fällt von deinen müden Füßen
die Samtsandale, die ich bin.

Dein großer Mantel läßt dich los.
Dein Blick, den ich mit meiner Wange
warm, wie mit einem Pfühl, empfange,
wird kommen, wird mich suchen, lange—
und legt beim Sonnenuntergange
sich fremden Steinen in den Schooß.

Was wirst du tun, Gott? Ich bin bange.

I, 36

What will you do, God, when I die?

I am your pitcher (when I shatter?)
I am your drink (when I go bitter?)
I, your garment; I, your craft.
Without me what reason have you?

Without me what house
where intimate words await you?
I, velvet sandal that falls from your foot.
I, cloak dropping from your shoulder.

Your gaze, which I welcome now
as it warms my cheek,
will search for me hour after hour
and lie at sunset, spent,
on an empty beach
among unfamiliar stones.

What will you do, God? It troubles me.

I, 36

An den jungen Bruder

Du, gestern Knabe, dem die Wirrnis kam:
Daß sich dein Blut in Blindheit nicht vergeude.
Du meinst nicht den Genuß, du meinst die Freude;
du bist gebildet als ein Bräutigam,
und deine Braut soll werden: deine Scham.

Die große Lust hat auch nach dir Verlangen,
und alle Arme sind auf einmal nackt.
Auf frommen Bildern sind die bleichen Wangen
von fremden Feuern überflackt;
und deine Sinne sind wie viele Schlangen,
die, von des Tones Rot umfangen,
sich spannen in der Tamburine Takt.

Und plötzlich bist du ganz allein gelassen
mit deinen Händen, die dich hassen—
und wenn dein Wille nicht ein Wunder tut:

Aber da gehen wie durch dunkle Gassen
von Gott Gerüchte durch dein dunkles Blut.

I, 38

(To the younger brother)

You, yesterday's boy,
to whom confusion came:
Listen, lest you forget who you are.

It was not pleasure you fell into. It was joy.
You were called to be bridegroom,
though the bride coming toward you is your shame.

What chose you is the great desire.
Now all flesh bares itself to you.

On pious images pale cheeks
blush with a strange fire.
Your senses uncoil like snakes
awakened by the beat of the tambourine.

Then suddenly you're left all alone
with your body that can't love you
and your will that can't save you.

But now, like a whispering in dark streets,
rumors of God run through your dark blood.

I, 38

An den jungen Bruder

Dann bete du, wie es dich dieser lehrt,
der selber aus der Wirrnis wiederkehrt
und so, daß er zu heiligen Gestalten,
die alle ihres Wesens Würde halten,
in einer Kirche und auf goldnen Smalten
die Schönheit malte, und sie hielt ein Schwert.

Er lehrt dich sagen:

Du mein tiefer Sinn,
vertraue mir, daß ich dich nicht enttäusche;
in meinem Blute sind so viel Geräusche,
ich aber weiß, daß ich aus Sehnsucht bin.

Ein großer Ernst bricht über mich herein.
In seinem Schatten ist das Leben kühl.
Ich bin zum erstenmal mit dir allein,

du, mein Gefühl . . .

I, 39

(To that younger brother)

Now pray,
as I who came back from the same confusion
learned to pray.

I returned to paint upon the altars
those old holy forms,
but they shone differently,
fierce in their beauty.

So now my prayer is this:

You, my own deep soul,
trust me. I will not betray you.
My blood is alive with many voices
telling me I am made of longing.

What mystery breaks over me now?
In its shadow I come into life.
For the first time I am alone with you—

you, my power to feel.

I, 39

Ich habe Hymnen, die ich schweige.
Es giebt ein Aufgerichtet sein,
darin ich meine Sinne neige:
du siehst mich groß und ich bin klein.
Du kannst mich dunkel unterscheiden
von jenen Dingen, welche knien;
sie sind wie Herden und sie weiden,
ich bin der Hirt am Hang der Heiden,
vor welchem sie zu Abend ziehn.
Dann komm ich hinter ihnen her
und höre dumpf die dunklen Brücken,
und in dem Rauch von ihren Rücken
verbirgt sich meine Wiederkehr.

I, 40

I have hymns you haven't heard.

There is an upward soaring
in which I bend close.
You can barely distinguish me
from the things that kneel before me.

They are like sheep, they are grazing.
I am the shepherd on the brow of the hill.
When evening draws them home
I follow after, the dark bridge thudding,

and the vapor rising from their backs
hides my own homecoming.

I, 40

Dein allererstes Wort war: *Licht:*
da ward die Zeit. Dann schwiegst du lange.
Dein zweites Wort ward Mensch und bange
(wir dunkeln noch in seinem Klange)
und wieder sinnt dein Angesicht.

Ich aber will dein drittes nicht.

Ich bete nachts oft: Sei der Stumme,
der wachsend in Gebärden bleibt
und den der Geist im Traume treibt,
daß er des Schweigens schwere Summe
in Stirnen und Gebirge schreibt.

Sei du die Zuflucht vor dem Zorne,
der das Unsagbare verstieß.
Es wurde Nacht im Paradies:
sei du der Hüter mit dem Horne,
und man erzählt nur, daß er blies.

I, 44

Your first word of all was *light*,
and time began. Then for long you were silent.

Your second word was man, and fear began,
which grips us still.

Are you about to speak again?
I don't want your third word.

Sometimes I pray: Please don't talk.
Let all your doing be by gesture only.
Go on writing in faces and stone
what your silence means.

Be our refuge from the wrath
that drove us out of Paradise.

Be our shepherd, but never call us—
we can't bear to know what's ahead.

I, 44

Du kommst und gehst. Die Türen fallen
viel sanfter zu, fast ohne Wehn.
Du bist der Leiseste von Allen,
die durch die leisen Häuser gehn.

Man kann sich so an dich gewöhnen,
daß man nicht aus dem Buche schaut,
wenn seine Bilder sich verschönen,
von deinem Schatten überblaut;
weil dich die Dinge immer tönen,
nur einmal leis und einmal laut.

Oft wenn ich dich in Sinnen sehe,
verteilt sich deine Allgestalt:
du gehst wie lauter lichte Rehe
und ich bin dunkel und bin Wald.

Du bist ein Rad, an dem ich stehe:
von deinen vielen dunklen Achsen
wird immer wieder eine schwer
und dreht sich näher zu mir her,
und meine willigen Werke wachsen
von Wiederkehr zu Wiederkehr.

I, 45

You come and go. The doors swing closed
ever more gently, almost without a shudder.
Of all who move through the quiet houses,
you are the quietest.

We become so accustomed to you,
we no longer look up
when your shadow falls over the book we are reading
and makes it glow. For all things
sing you: at times
we just hear them more clearly.

Often when I imagine you
your wholeness cascades into many shapes.
You run like a herd of luminous deer
and I am dark, I am forest.

You are a wheel at which I stand,
whose dark spokes sometimes catch me up,
revolve me nearer to the center.
Then all the work I put my hand to
widens from turn to turn.

I, 45

Ihr vielen unbestürmten Städte,
habt ihr euch nie den Feind ersehnt?
O daß er euch belagert hätte
ein langes schwankendes Jahrzehnt.

Bis ihr ihn trostlos und in Trauern,
bis daß ihr hungernd ihn ertrugt;
er liegt wie Landschaft vor den Mauern,
denn also weiß er auszudauern
um jene, die er heimgesucht.

Schaut aus vom Rande eurer Dächer
da lagert er und wird nicht matt
und wird nicht weniger und schwächer
und schickt nicht Droher und Versprecher
und Überreder in die Stadt.

Er ist der große Mauerbrecher,
der eine stumme Arbeit hat.

I, 49

You many unassaulted cities:
Have you never yearned for the enemy?
Yearned that he might besiege you
for long irresolute years, until

in hopelessness and hunger you receive him?
He extends like the land beyond your walls,
and he knows he can hold out longer.

Look from your balconies:
there he camps. He does not tire
or diminish in size or strength.
He sends no messengers to threaten
or to promise or persuade.

He who will overcome you
is working in silence.

I, 49

Ich komme aus meinen Schwingen heim,
mit denen ich mich verlor.
Ich war Gesang, und Gott, der Reim,
rauscht noch in meinem Ohr.

Ich werde wieder still und schlicht,
und meine Stimme steht;
es senkte sich mein Angesicht
zu besserem Gebet.
Den andern war ich wie ein Wind,
da ich sie rüttelnd rief.
Weit war ich, wo die Engel sind,
hoch, wo das Licht in Nichts zerrinnt—
Gott aber dunkelt tief . . .

I, 50

I come home from the soaring
in which I lost myself.
I was song, and the refrain which is God
is still roaring in my ears.

Now I am still
and plain:
no more words.

To the others I was like a wind:
I made them shake.
I'd gone very far, as far as the angels,
and high, where light thins into nothing.

But deep in the darkness is God . . .

I, 50

Du wirst nur mit der Tat erfaßt;
mit Händen nur erhellt;
ein jeder Sinn ist nur ein Gast
und sehnt sich aus der Welt.

Ersonnen ist ein jeder Sinn,
man fühlt den feinen Saum darin
und daß ihn einer spann:
Du aber kommst und giebst dich hin
und fällst den Flüchtling an.

Ich will nicht wissen, wo du bist,
sprich mir aus überall.
Dein williger Euangelist
verzeichnet alles und vergißt
zu schauen nach dem Schall.

Ich geh doch immer auf dich zu
mit meinem ganzen Gehn . . .

I, 51

Only in our doing can we grasp you.
Only with our hands can we illumine you.
The mind is but a visitor:
it thinks us out of our world.

Each mind fabricates itself.
We sense its limits, for we have made them.
And just when we would flee them, you come
and make of yourself an offering.

I don't want to think a place for you.
Speak to me from everywhere.
Your Gospel can be comprehended
without looking for its source.

When I go toward you
it is with my whole life.

I, 51

Mein Leben hat das gleiche Kleid und Haar
wie aller alten Zaren Sterbestunde.
Die Macht entfremdete nur meinem Munde,
doch meine Reiche, die ich schweigend runde,
versammeln sich in meinem Hintergrunde
und meine Sinne sind noch Gossudar.

Für sie ist beten immer noch: Erbauen,
aus allen Maßen bauen, daß das Grauen
fast wie die Größe wird und schön,—
und: jedes Hinknien und Vertrauen
(daß es die andern nicht beschauen)
mit vielen goldenen und blauen
und bunten Kuppeln überhöhn . . .

I, 52

My life bedecks itself no differently
from the deathbeds of the ancient czars.
It's only their power I cannot claim.
I keep my own empires in the background
and manage them in silence.

Their prayer is always: Build,
use everything, build, so terror
may be turned to bigness and even beauty.
And, so that others do not see our fear,
let every kneeling and every pious gesture
be overarched with splendor—
domes, dazzling gold and blue.

I, 52

Und Gott befiehlt mir, daß ich schriebe:

Den Königen sei Grausamkeit.
Sie ist der Engel vor der Liebe,
und ohne diesen Bogen bliebe
mir keine Brücke in die Zeit.

Und Gott befiehlt mir, daß ich male:

Die Zeit ist mir mein tiefstes Weh,
so legte ich in ihre Schale:
das wache Weib, die Wundenmale,
den reichen Tod (daß er sie zahle),
der Städte bange Bacchanale,
den Wahnsinn und die Könige.

Und Gott befiehlt mir, daß ich baue:

Denn König bin ich von der Zeit.
Dir aber bin ich nur der graue
Mitwisser deiner Einsamkeit.
Und bin das Auge mit der Braue . . .

Das über meine Schulter schaue
von Ewigkeit zu Ewigkeit.

I, 53

And God said to me, Write:

> Leave the cruelty to kings.
> Without that angel barring the way to love
> there would be no bridge for me
> into time.

And God said to me, Paint:

> Time is the canvas
> stretched by my pain:
> the watchful woman,
> the wounds of Christ,
> the city's sad bacchanals,
> the madness of kings.

And God said to me, Go forth:

> For I am king of time.
> But to you I am only the shadowy one
> who knows with you your loneliness
> and sees through your eyes.

He sees through my eyes
in all the ages.

I, 53

Die Dichter haben dich verstreut
(es ging ein Sturm durch alles Stammeln),
ich aber will dich wieder sammeln
in dem Gefäß, das dich erfreut.

Ich wanderte in vielem Winde;
da triebst du tausendmal darin.
Ich bringe alles was ich finde:
als Becher brauchte dich der Blinde,
sehr tief verbarg dich das Gesinde,
der Bettler aber hielt dich hin;
und manchmal war bei einem Kinde
ein großes Stück von deinem Sinn.

Du siehst, daß ich ein Sucher bin.

Einer, der hinter seinen Händen
verborgen geht und wie ein Hirt;
(mögst du den Blick der ihn beirrt,
den Blick der Fremden von ihm wenden).
Einer der träumt, dich zu vollenden
und: daß er sich vollenden wird.

I, 55

The poets have scattered you.
A storm ripped through the stammering.
I want to gather you up again
in a vessel that makes you glad.

I wander in the thousand winds
that you are churning,
and bring back everything I find.

The blind man needed you as a cup.
The servant concealed you.
The beggar held you out as I passed.

You see, I am one who likes to look for things.

I am one who, barely noticed,
like a shepherd,
comes up from behind . . .
One who dreams of making you complete,
and in that way completes himself.

I, 55

Gott spricht zu jedem nur, eh er ihn macht,
dann geht er schweigend mit ihm aus der Nacht.
Aber die Worte, eh jeder beginnt,
diese wolkigen Worte, sind:

Von deinen Sinnen hinausgesandt,
geh bis an deiner Sehnsucht Rand;
gieb mir Gewand.
Hinter den Dingen wachse als Brand,
daß ihre Schatten, ausgespannt,
immer mich ganz bedecken.

Laß dir Alles geschehn: Schönheit und Schrecken.
Man muß nur gehn: Kein Gefühl ist das fernste.
Laß dich von mir nicht trennen.
Nah ist das Land,
das sie das Leben nennen.

Du wirst es erkennen
an seinem Ernste.

Gieb mir die Hand.

I, 59

God speaks to each of us as he makes us,
then walks with us silently out of the night.

These are the words we dimly hear:

You, sent out beyond your recall,
go to the limits of your longing.
Embody me.

Flare up like flame
and make big shadows I can move in.

Let everything happen to you: beauty and terror.
Just keep going. No feeling is final.
Don't let yourself lose me.

Nearby is the country they call life.
You will know it by its seriousness.

Give me your hand.

I, 59

Ich war bei den ältesten Mönchen, den Malern und
    Mythenmeldern,
die schrieben ruhig Geschichten und zeichneten Runen
    des Ruhms.
Und ich seh dich in meinen Gesichten mit Winden,
    Wassern und Wäldern
rauschend am Rande des Christentums,
du Land, nicht zu lichten.

Ich will dich erzählen, ich will dich beschaun und
    beschreiben,
nicht mit Bol und mit Gold, nur mit Tinte aus
    Apfelbaumrinden;
ich kann auch mit Perlen dich nicht an die Blätter binden,
und das zitterndste Bild, das mir meine Sinne erfinden,
du würdest es blind durch dein einfaches Sein übertreiben.

So will ich die Dinge in dir nur bescheiden und schlichthin
    benamen,
will die Könige nennen, die ältesten, woher sie kamen,
und will ihre Taten und Schlachten berichten am Rand
    meiner Seiten.

I was there with the first mythmakers and monks
who made up your stories, traced your runes.

But now I see you:
wind, woods, and water,
roaring at the rim of Christendom—
you, land,
to be left in darkness.

I want to utter you. I want to portray you
not with lapis or gold, but with colors made of
     apple bark.
There is no image I could invent
that your presence would not eclipse.

I want, then, simply
to say the names of things.
I'll leave aside kings and their lineages,
their deeds and battles.

Denn du bist der Boden. Dir sind nur wie Sommer die
    Zeiten,
und du denkst an die nahen nicht anders als an die
    entfernten,
und ob sie dich tiefer besamen und besser bebauen lernten:
du fühlst dich nur leise berührt von den ähnlichen Ernten
und hörst weder Säer noch Schnitter, die über dich
    schreiten.

I, 60

For you are the ground.
The ages to you are only seasons.

You look on the near no differently from the far,
and if they've learned to plant you more deeply
or build more grandly upon you,

you barely feel it. You hear
neither sower nor reaper
when their footsteps pass over you.

I, 60

Du dunkelnder Grund, geduldig erträgst du die Mauern.
Und vielleicht erlaubst du noch eine Stunde den Städten
    zu dauern
und gewährst noch zwei Stunden den Kirchen und ein-
    samen Klöstern
und lässest fünf Stunden noch Mühsal allen Erlöstern
und siehst noch sieben Stunden das Tagwerk des Bauern—:

Eh du wieder Wald wirst und Wasser und wachsende
    Wildnis
in der Stunde der unerfaßlichen Angst,
da du dein unvollendetes Bildnis
von allen Dingen zurückverlangst.

Gieb mir noch eine kleine Weile Zeit: ich will die Dinge
so wie keiner lieben
bis sie dir alle würdig sind und weit.

Ich will nur sieben Tage, sieben
auf die sich keiner noch geschrieben,
sieben Seiten Einsamkeit.

Dear darkening ground,
you've endured so patiently the walls we've built,
perhaps you'll give the cities one more hour

and grant the churches and cloisters two.
And those that labor—will you let their work
grip them another five hours, or seven,

before you become forest again, and water, and widening
        wilderness
in that hour of inconceivable terror
when you take back your name
from all things.

Just give me a little more time!
I want to love the things
as no one has thought to love them,
until they're worthy of you and real.

I want only seven days, seven
on which no one has ever written himself—
seven pages of solitude.

Wem du das Buch giebst, welches die umfaßt,
der wird gebückt über den Blättern bleiben.
Es sei denn, daß du ihn in Händen hast,
um selbst zu schreiben.

I, 61

There will be a book that includes these pages,
and the one who takes it in his hands
will long sit staring at it,
until he feels you holding him
and writing through him.

I, 61

So bin ich nur als Kind erwacht,
so sicher im Vertraun
nach jeder Angst und jeder Nacht
dich wieder anzuschaun.
Ich weiß, sooft mein Denken mißt,
wie tief, wie lang, wie weit—:
du aber bist und bist und bist,
umzittert von der Zeit.

Mir ist, als wär ich jetzt zugleich
Kind, Knab und Mann und mehr.
Ich fühle: nur der Ring ist reich
durch seine Wiederkehr.

Ich danke dir, du tiefe Kraft,
die immer leiser mit mir schafft
wie hinter vielen Wänden;
jetzt ward mir erst der Werktag schlicht
und wie ein heiliges Gesicht
zu meinen dunklen Händen.

I, 62

Only as a child am I awake
and able to trust
that after every fear and every night
I will behold you again.

However often I get lost,
however far my thinking strays,
I know you will be here, right here,
time trembling around you.

To me it is as if I were at once
infant, boy, man and more.
I feel that only as it circles
is abundance found.

I thank you, deep power
that works me ever more lightly
in ways I can't make out.
The day's labor grows simple now,
and like a holy face
held in my dark hands.

I, 62

The Book of
PILGRIMAGE

Dich wundert nicht des Sturmes Wucht,—
du hast ihn wachsen sehn;—
die Bäume flüchten. Ihre Flucht
schafft schreitende Alleen.
Da weißt du, der vor dem sie fliehn
ist der, zu dem du gehst,
und deine Sinne singen ihn,
wenn du am Fenster stehst.

Des Sommers Wochen standen still,
es stieg der Bäume Blut;
jetzt fühlst du, daß es fallen will
in den der Alles tut.
Du glaubtest schon erkannt die Kraft,
als du die Frucht erfaßt,
jetzt wird sie wieder rätselhaft,
und du bist wieder Gast.

Der Sommer war so wie dein Haus,
drin weißt du alles stehn—
jetzt mußt du in dein Herz hinaus
wie in die Ebene gehn.
Die große Einsamkeit beginnt,
die Tage werden taub,
aus deinen Sinnen nimmt der Wind
die Welt wie welkes Laub.

You are not surprised at the force of the storm—
you have seen it growing.
The trees flee. Their flight
sets the boulevards streaming. And you know:
he whom they flee is the one
you move toward. All your senses
sing him, as you stand at the window.

The weeks stood still in summer.
The trees' blood rose. Now you feel
it wants to sink back
into the source of everything. You thought
you could trust that power
when you plucked the fruit;
now it becomes a riddle again,
and you again a stranger.

Summer was like your house: you knew
where each thing stood.
Now you must go out into your heart
as onto a vast plain. Now
the immense loneliness begins.

The days go numb, the wind
sucks the world from your senses like withered leaves.

Durch ihre leeren Zweige sieht
der Himmel, den du hast;
sei Erde jetzt und Abendlied
und Land, darauf er paßt.
Demütig sei jetzt wie ein Ding,
zu Wirklichkeit gereift,—
daß Der, von dem die Kunde ging,
dich fühlt, wenn er dich greift.

II, 1

Through the empty branches the sky remains.
It is what you have.
Be earth now, and evensong.
Be the ground lying under that sky.
Be modest now, like a thing
ripened until it is real,
so that he who began it all
can feel you when he reaches for you.

II, 1

Ich bete wieder, du Erlauchter,
du hörst mich wieder durch den Wind,
weil meine Tiefen niegebrauchter
rauschender Worte mächtig sind.

Ich war zerstreut; an Widersacher
in Stücken war verteilt mein Ich.
O Gott, mich lachten alle Lacher
und alle Trinker tranken mich.

In Höfen hab ich mich gesammelt
aus Abfall und aus altem Glas,
mit halbem Mund dich angestammelt,
dich, Ewiger aus Ebenmaß.
Wie hob ich meine halben Hände
zu dir in namenlosem Flehn,
daß ich die Augen wiederfände,
mit denen ich dich angesehn.

Ich war ein Haus nach einem Brand,
darin nur Mörder manchmal schlafen,
eh ihre hungerigen Strafen
sie weiterjagen in das Land;

I am praying again, Awesome One.

You hear me again, as words
from the depths of me
rush toward you in the wind.

I've been scattered in pieces,
torn by conflict,
mocked by laughter,
washed down in drink.

In alleyways I sweep myself up
out of garbage and broken glass.
With my half-mouth I stammer you,
who are eternal in your symmetry.
I lift to you my half-hands
in wordless beseeching, that I may find again
the eyes with which I once beheld you.

I am a house gutted by fire
where only the guilty sometimes sleep
before the punishment that devours them
hounds them out into the open.

ich war wie eine Stadt am Meer,
wenn eine Seuche sie bedrängte,
die sich wie eine Leiche schwer
den Kindern an die Hände hängte.

Ich war mir fremd wie irgendwer,
und wußte nur von ihm, daß er
einst meine junge Mutter kränkte
als sie mich trug . . .

Jetzt bin ich wieder aufgebaut
aus allen Stücken meiner Schande,
und sehne mich nach einem Bande,
nach einem einigen Verstande,
der mich wie ein Ding überschaut,—
nach deines Herzens großen Händen—
(o kämen sie doch auf mich zu).
Ich zähle mich, mein Gott, und du,
du hast das Recht, mich zu verschwenden.

II, 2

I am a city by the sea
sinking into a toxic tide.
I am strange to myself, as though someone unknown
had poisoned my mother as she carried me.

It's here in all the pieces of my shame
that now I find myself again.
I yearn to belong to something, to be contained
in an all-embracing mind that sees me
as a single thing.
I yearn to be held
in the great hands of your heart—
oh let them take me now.

Into them I place these fragments, my life,
and you, God—spend them however you want.

II, 2

Ich bin derselbe noch, der kniete
vor dir in mönchischem Gewand:
der tiefe, dienende Levite,
den du erfüllt, der dich erfand.
Die Stimme einer stillen Zelle,
an der die Welt vorüberweht,—
und du bist immer noch die Welle
die über alle Dinge geht.

Es ist nichts andres. Nur ein Meer,
aus dem die Länder manchmal steigen.
Es ist nichts andres denn ein Schweigen
von schönen Engeln und von Geigen,
und der Verschwiegene ist der,
zu dem sich alle Dinge neigen,
von seiner Stärke Strahlen schwer.

Bist du denn Alles,—ich der Eine,
der sich ergiebt und sich empört?
Bin ich denn nicht das Allgemeine,
bin ich nicht Alles, wenn ich weine,
und du der Eine, der es hört?

Hörst du denn etwas neben mir?
Sind da noch Stimmen außer meiner?
Ist da ein Sturm? Auch ich bin einer,
und meine Wälder winken dir.

I'm still the one who knelt before you
in monks' robes, wanting to be of use.
You filled him as he called you into being—
a voice from a quiet cell
with the world blowing past.
And you are ever again the wave
sweeping through all things.

That's all there is. Only an ocean
where now and again islands appear.
That's all there is: no harps, no angels.
And the one before whom all things bow
is the one without a voice.

Are you, then, the All? and I the separated one
who tumbles and rages?
Am I not the whole? Am I not all things
when I weep, and you the single one, who hears it?

Listen—don't you hear something?
Aren't there voices other than mine?
Is that a storm? I am one also,
whipping the trees to call to you.

Ist da ein Lied, ein krankes, kleines,
das dich am Micherhören stört,—
auch ich bin eines, höre meines,
das einsam ist und unerhört.

Ich bin derselbe noch, der bange
dich manchmal fragte, wer du seist.
Nach jedem Sonnenuntergange
bin ich verwundet und verwaist,
ein blasser Allem Abgelöster
und ein Verschmähter jeder Schar,
und alle Dinge stehn wie Klöster,
in denen ich gefangen war.
Dann brauch ich dich, du Eingeweihter,
du sanfter Nachbar jeder Not,
du meines Leidens leiser Zweiter,
du Gott, dann brauch ich dich wie Brot.
Du weißt vielleicht nicht, wie die Nächte
für Menschen, die nicht schlafen, sind:
da sind sie alle Ungerechte,
der Greis, die Jungfrau und das Kind.
Sie fahren auf wie totgesagt,
von schwarzen Dingen nah umgeben,
und ihre weißen Hände beben,
verwoben in ein wildes Leben
wie Hunde in ein Bild der Jagd.
Vergangenes steht noch bevor,
und in der Zukunft liegen Leichen,
ein Mann im Mantel pocht am Tor,
und mit dem Auge und dem Ohr

Are you distracted from hearing me
by some whining little tune?
That's mine as well—hear mine as well;
it's lonely and unheard.

I'm the one who's been asking you—
it hurts to ask—Who are you?
I am orphaned
each time the sun goes down.
I can feel cast out from everything
and even churches look like prisons.

That's when I want you—
you knower of my emptiness,
you unspeaking partner to my sorrow—
that's when I need you, God, like food.

Maybe you don't know what the nights are like
for people who can't sleep.
They all feel guilty—
the old man, the young woman, the child.
They're driven through darkness as though condemned,
their pale hands writhing; they're twisted
like a pack of frenzied hounds.

What's past lies still ahead,
and the future is finished.

ist noch kein erstes Morgenzeichen,
kein Hahnruf ist noch zu erreichen.
Die Nacht ist wie ein großes Haus.
Und mit der Angst der wunden Hände
reißen sie Türen in die Wände,—
dann kommen Gänge ohne Ende,
und nirgends ist ein Tor hinaus.

Und so, mein Gott, ist jede Nacht;
immer sind welche aufgewacht,
die gehn und gehn und dich nicht finden.
Hörst du sie mit dem Schritt von Blinden
das Dunkel treten?
Auf Treppen, die sich niederwinden,
hörst du sie beten?
Hörst du sie fallen auf den schwarzen Steinen?
Du mußt sie weinen hören; denn sie weinen.

Ich suche dich, weil sie vorübergehn
an meiner Tür. Ich kann sie beinah sehn.
Wen soll ich rufen, wenn nicht den,
der dunkel ist und nächtiger als Nacht.
Den Einzigen, der ohne Lampe wacht
und doch nicht bangt; den Tiefen, den das Licht
noch nicht verwöhnt hat und von dem ich weiß,
weil er mit Bäumen aus der Erde bricht
und weil er leis
als Duft in mein gesenktes Angesicht
aus Erde steigt.

II, 3

They see not the faintest glimmer of morning
and listen in vain for the cock's crow.
The night is a huge house
where doors torn open by terrified hands
lead into endless corridors, and there's no way out.

God, every night is like that.
Always there are some awake,
who turn, turn, and do not find you.
Don't you hear them blindly treading the dark?
Don't you hear them crying out
as they go farther and farther down?
Surely you hear them weep; for they are weeping.

I seek you, because they are passing
right by my door. Whom should I turn to,
if not the one whose darkness
is darker than night, the only one
who keeps vigil with no candle,
and is not afraid—
the deep one, whose being I trust,
for it breaks through the earth into trees,
and rises,
when I bow my head,
faint as a fragrance
from the soil.

II, 3

Du Ewiger, du hast dich mir gezeigt.
Ich liebe dich wie einen lieben Sohn,
der mich einmal verlassen hat als Kind,
weil ihn das Schicksal rief auf einen Thron,
vor dem die Länder alle Täler sind.
Ich bin zurückgeblieben wie ein Greis,
der seinen großen Sohn nichtmehr versteht
und wenig von den neuen Dingen weiß,
zu welchen seines Samens Wille geht.
Ich bebe manchmal für dein tiefes Glück,
das auf so vielen fremden Schiffen fährt,
ich wünsche manchmal dich in mich zurück,
in dieses Dunkel, das dich großgenährt.
Ich bange manchmal, daß du nichtmehr bist,
wenn ich mich sehr verliere an die Zeit.
Dann les ich von dir: der Euangelist
schreibt überall von deiner Ewigkeit.

Unending one, you've shown yourself to me.

I love you as I would love a son
who long since went from me,
because his fate called him
to a high place
where he could see out
over all things.

I have stayed home like an old man
who no longer understands his son
and knows little of the new things
that concern him now.

I tremble sometimes for your happiness,
that ventures abroad on so many ships.
I wish sometimes that you were back inside me,
in this darkness that grew you.

And when I get confused by time,
I fear you no longer exist—
though I know, the Evangelist
keeps writing about your eternity.

Ich bin der Vater; doch der Sohn ist mehr,
ist alles, was der Vater war, und der,
der er nicht wurde, wird in jenem groß;
er ist die Zukunft und die Wiederkehr,
er ist der Schooß, er ist das Meer . . .

II, 4

I am the father; but the son is more.
He is all the father was, and what the father was not
grows great in him. He is the future
and the return. He is the womb, he is the sea . . .

II, 4

Dir ist mein Beten keine Blasphemie:
als schlüge ich in alten Büchern nach,
daß ich dir sehr verwandt bin—tausendfach.

Ich will dir Liebe geben. Die und die. . . .

Liebt man denn einen Vater? Geht man nicht,
wie du von mir gingst, Härte im Gesicht,
von seinen hülflos leeren Händen fort?
Legt man nicht leise sein verwelktes Wort
in alte Bücher, die man selten liest?
Fließt man nicht wie von einer Wasserscheide
von seinem Herzen ab zu Lust und Leide?
Ist uns der Vater denn nicht das, was war;
vergangne Jahre, welche fremd gedacht,
veraltete Gebärde, tote Tracht,
verblühte Hände und verblichnes Haar?
Und war er selbst für seine Zeit ein Held,
er ist das Blatt, das, wenn wir wachsen, fällt.

II, 5

To you my prayers are no blasphemy:
the old books tell me I am related to you
in a thousand ways.

I want to love you.

Does anyone love a father? Doesn't one turn away
as you turned from me, your face hardened,
wanting to escape these empty, helpless hands?
Doesn't one leave a father's worn-out words
to old books that are seldom read?

Is his heart not a watershed
from which one flows away,
toward passion and suffering?

Isn't the father always that which was?
Used-up years with their odd ways of thinking,
outmoded gestures, old-fashioned dress,
pale hands and ashen hair.

And while in his time he may have been a hero,
he is a leaf that, when we grow, falls away.

II, 5

Und seine Sorgfalt ist uns wie ein Alb,
und seine Stimme ist uns wie ein Stein,—
wir möchten seiner Rede hörig sein,
aber wir hören seine Worte halb.
Das große Drama zwischen ihm und uns
lärmt viel zu laut, einander zu verstehn,
wir sehen nur die Formen seines Munds,
aus denen Silben fallen, die vergehn.
So sind wir noch viel ferner ihm als fern,
wenn auch die Liebe uns noch weit verwebt,
erst wenn er sterben muß auf diesem Stern,
sehn wir, daß er auf diesem Stern gelebt.

Das ist der Vater uns. Und ich—ich soll
dich Vater nennen?
Das hieße tausendmal mich von dir trennen.
Du bist mein Sohn. Ich werde dich erkennen,
wie man sein einzigliebes Kind erkennt, auch dann,
wenn es ein Mann geworden ist, ein alter Mann.

II, 6

His caring is a nightmare to us,
and his voice a stone.

We would like to heed his words,
but we only half hear them.
The big drama between us
makes too much noise
for us to understand each other.

We watch his lips moving,
shaping sounds that die away.
We feel endlessly distant,
though we are endlessly bound by love.
Only when we notice that he is dying
do we know he lived.

That is Father to us. And I—
I should call you Father?
That would open a gulf between us.
You are my son.

I will know you
as one knows his only beloved child,
even when he has become a man,
an aging man.

II, 6

Du bist der Erbe.
Söhne sind die Erben,
denn Väter sterben.
Söhne stehn und blühn.
Du bist der Erbe.

II, 9

So God, you are the one
who comes after.

It is sons who inherit,
while fathers die.
Sons stand and bloom.

You are the heir.

II, 9

Und du erbst das Grün
vergangner Gärten und das stille Blau
zerfallner Himmel.
Tau aus tausend Tagen,
die vielen Sommer, die die Sonnen sagen,
und lauter Frühlinge mit Glanz und Klagen
wie viele Briefe einer jungen Frau.
Du erbst die Herbste, die wie Prunkgewänder
in der Erinnerung von Dichtern liegen,
und alle Winter, wie verwaiste Länder,
scheinen sich leise an dich anzuschmiegen.
Du erbst Venedig und Kasan und Rom,
Florenz wird dein sein, der Pisaner Dom,
die Troïtzka Lawra und das Monastir,
das unter Kiews Gärten ein Gewirr
von Gängen bildet, dunkel und verschlungen, —
Moskau mit Glocken wie Erinnerungen, —
und Klang wird dein sein Geigen, Hörner, Zungen,
und jedes Lied, das tief genug erklungen,
wird an dir glänzen wie ein Edelstein.

And you inherit the green
of vanished gardens
and the motionless blue of fallen skies,
dew of a thousand dawns, countless summers
the suns sang, and springtimes to break your heart
like a young woman's letters.

You inherit the autumns, folded like festive clothing
in the memories of poets; and all the winters,
like abandoned fields, bequeath you their quietness.
You inherit Venice, Kazan, and Rome;

Florence will be yours, and Pisa's cathedral,
Moscow with bells like memories,
and the Troiska convent, and that monastery
whose maze of tunnels lies swallowed under Kiev's gardens.

Sound will be yours, of string and brass and reed,
and sometimes the songs will seem
to come from inside you.

Für dich nur schließen sich die Dichter ein
und sammeln Bilder, rauschende und reiche,
und gehn hinaus und reifen durch Vergleiche
und sind ihr ganzes Leben so allein . . .
Und Maler malen ihre Bilder nur,
damit du unvergänglich die Natur,
die du vergänglich schufst, zurückempfängst:
alles wird ewig. Sieh, das Weib ist längst
in der Madonna Lisa reif wie Wein;
es müßte nie ein Weib mehr sein,
denn Neues bringt kein neues Weib hinzu.
Die, welche bilden, sind wie du.
Sie wollen Ewigkeit. Sie sagen: Stein,
sei ewig. Und das heißt: sei dein!

Und auch, die lieben, sammeln für dich ein:
Sie sind die Dichter einer kurzen Stunde,
sie küssen einem ausdruckslosen Munde
ein Lächeln auf, als formten sie ihn schöner,
und bringen Lust und sind die Angewöhner
zu Schmerzen, welche erst erwachsen machen.
Sie bringen Leiden mit in ihrem Lachen,
Sehnsüchte, welche schlafen, und erwachen,
um aufzuweinen in der fremden Brust.

For your sake poets sequester themselves,
gather images to churn the mind,
journey forth, ripening with metaphor,
and all their lives they are so alone. . . .
And painters paint their pictures only
that the world, so transient as you made it,
can be given back to you,
to last forever.

All becomes eternal. See: In the Mona Lisa
some woman has long since ripened like wine,
and the enduring feminine is held there
through all the ages.

Those who create are like you.
They long for the eternal.
They say, Stone, be forever!
And that means: be yours.

And lovers also gather your inheritance.
They are the poets of one brief hour.
They kiss an expressionless mouth into a smile
as if creating it anew, more beautiful.

Awakening desire, they make a place
where pain can enter;
that's how growing happens.
They bring suffering along with their laughter,
and longings that had slept and now awaken
to weep in a stranger's arms.

Sie häufen Rätselhaftes an und sterben,
wie Tiere sterben, ohne zu begreifen,—
aber sie werden vielleicht Enkel haben,
in denen ihre grünen Leben reifen;
durch diese wirst du jene Liebe erben,
die sie sich blind und wie im Schlafe gaben.

So fließt der Dinge Überfluß dir zu.
Und wie die obern Becken von Fontänen
beständig überströmen, wie von Strähnen
gelösten Haares, in die tiefste Schale,—
so fällt die Fülle dir in deine Tale,
wenn Dinge und Gedanken übergehn.

II, 10

They let the riddles pile up and then they die
the way animals die, without making sense of it.
But maybe in those who come after,
their green life will ripen;
it's then that you will inherit the love
to which they gave themselves so blindly, as in a sleep.

Thus the overflow from things
pours into you.
Just as a fountain's higher basins
spill down like strands of loosened hair
into the lowest vessel,
so streams the fullness into you,
when things and thoughts cannot contain it.

II, 10

Lösch mir die Augen aus: ich kann dich sehn,
wirf mir die Ohren zu: ich kann dich hören,
und ohne Füße kann ich zu dir gehn,
und ohne Mund noch kann ich dich beschwören.
Brich mir die Arme ab, ich fasse dich
mit meinem Herzen wie mit einer Hand,
halt mir das Herz zu, und mein Hirn wird schlagen,
und wirfst du in mein Hirn den Brand,
so werd ich dich auf meinem Blute tragen.

II, 7

Extinguish my eyes, I'll go on seeing you.
Seal my ears, I'll go on hearing you.
And without feet I can make my way to you,
without a mouth I can swear your name.

Break off my arms, I'll take hold of you
with my heart as with a hand.
Stop my heart, and my brain will start to beat.
And if you consume my brain with fire,
I'll feel you burn in every drop of my blood.

II, 7

. . . Keiner lebt sein Leben.
Zufälle sind die Menschen, Stimmen, Stücke,
Alltage, Ängste, viele kleine Glücke,
verkleidet schon als Kinder, eingemummt,
als Masken mündig, als Gesicht—verstummt.

Ich denke oft: Schatzhäuser müssen sein,
wo alle diese vielen Leben liegen
wie Panzer oder Sänften oder Wiegen,
in welche nie ein Wirklicher gestiegen,
und wie Gewänder, welche ganz allein
nicht stehen können und sich sinkend schmiegen
an starke Wände aus gewölbtem Stein.

Und wenn ich abends immer weiterginge
aus meinem Garten, drin ich müde bin,—
ich weiß: dann führen alle Wege hin
zum Arsenal der ungelebten Dinge . . .

II, 11

No one lives his life.

Disguised since childhood,
haphazardly assembled
from voices and fears and little pleasures,
we come of age as masks.

Our true face never speaks.

Somewhere there must be storehouses
where all these lives are laid away
like suits of armor or old carriages
or clothes hanging limply on the walls.

Maybe all paths lead there,
to the repository of unlived things.

II, 11

Und doch, obwohl ein jeder von sich strebt
wie aus dem Kerker, der ihn haßt und hält,—
es ist ein großes Wunder in der Welt:
ich fühle: alles Leben wird gelebt.

Wer lebt es denn? Sind das die Dinge, die
wie eine ungespielte Melodie
im Abend wie in einer Harfe stehn?
Sind das die Winde, die von Wassern wehn,
sind das die Zweige, die sich Zeichen geben,
sind das die Blumen, die die Düfte weben,
sind das die langen alternden Alleen?
Sind das die warmen Tiere, welche gehn,
sind das die Vögel, die sich fremd erheben?

Wer lebt es denn? Lebst du es, Gott,—das Leben?

II, 12

And yet, though we strain
against the deadening grip
of daily necessity,
I sense there is this mystery:

All life is being lived.

Who is living it, then?
Is it the things themselves,
or something waiting inside them,
like an unplayed melody in a flute?

Is it the winds blowing over the waters?
Is it the branches that signal to each other?

Is it flowers
interweaving their fragrances,
or streets, as they wind through time?

Is it the animals, warmly moving,
or the birds, that suddenly rise up?

Who lives it, then? God, are you the one
who is living life?

II, 12

Alle, welche dich suchen, versuchen dich.
Und die, so dich finden, binden dich
an Bild und Gebärde.

Ich aber will dich begreifen
wie dich die Erde begreift;
mit meinem Reifen
reift
dein Reich.

Ich will von dir keine Eitelkeit,
die dich beweist.
Ich weiß, daß die Zeit
anders heißt
als du.

Tu mir kein Wunder zulieb.
Gieb deinen Gesetzen recht,
die von Geschlecht zu Geschlecht
sichtbarer sind.

II, 15

All who seek you
test you.
And those who find you
bind you to image and gesture.

I would rather sense you
as the earth senses you.
In my ripening
ripens
what you are.

I need from you no tricks
to prove you exist.
Time, I know,
is other than you.

No miracles, please.
Just let your laws
become clearer
from generation to generation.

II, 15

Wenn etwas mir vom Fenster fällt
(und wenn es auch das Kleinste wäre)
wie stürzt sich das Gesetz der Schwere
gewaltig wie ein Wind vom Meere
auf jeden Ball und jede Beere
und trägt sie in den Kern der Welt.

Ein jedes Ding ist überwacht
von einer flugbereiten Güte
wie jeder Stein und jede Blüte
und jedes kleine Kind bei Nacht.
Nur wir, in unsrer Hoffahrt, drängen
aus einigen Zusammenhängen
in einer Freiheit leeren Raum,
statt, klugen Kräften hingegeben,
uns aufzuheben wie ein Baum.
Statt in die weitesten Geleise
sich still und willig einzureihn,
verknüpft man sich auf manche Weise,—
und wer sich ausschließt jedem Kreise,
ist jetzt so namenlos allein.

Da muß er lernen von den Dingen,
anfangen wieder wie ein Kind,
weil sie, die Gott am Herzen hingen,
nicht von ihm fortgegangen sind.

How surely gravity's law,
strong as an ocean current,
takes hold of even the smallest thing
and pulls it toward the heart of the world.

Each thing—
each stone, blossom, child—
is held in place.
Only we, in our arrogance,
push out beyond what we each belong to
for some empty freedom.

If we surrendered
to earth's intelligence
we could rise up rooted, like trees.

Instead we entangle ourselves
in knots of our own making
and struggle, lonely and confused.

So, like children, we begin again
to learn from the things,
because they are in God's heart;
they have never left him.

Eins muß er wieder können: fallen,
geduldig in der Schwere ruhn,
der sich vermaß, den Vögeln allen
im Fliegen es zuvorzutun . . .

II, 16

This is what the things can teach us:
to fall,
patiently to trust our heaviness.
Even a bird has to do that
before he can fly.

II, 16

Manchmal steht einer auf beim Abendbrot
und geht hinaus und geht und geht und geht,—
weil eine Kirche wo im Osten steht.

Und seine Kinder segnen ihn wie tot.

Und einer, welcher stirbt in seinem Haus,
bleibt drinnen wohnen, bleibt in Tisch und Glas,
so daß die Kinder in die Welt hinaus
zu jener Kirche ziehn, die er vergaß.

II, 19

Sometimes a man rises from the supper table
and goes outside. And he keeps on going
because somewhere to the east there's a church.
His children bless his name as if he were dead.

Another man stays at home until he dies,
stays with plates and glasses.
So then it is his children who go out
into the world, seeking the church that he forgot.

II, 19

Du bist die Zukunft, großes Morgenrot
über den Ebenen der Ewigkeit.
Du bist der Hahnschrei nach der Nacht der Zeit,
der Tau, die Morgenmette und die Maid,
der fremde Mann, die Mutter und der Tod.

Du bist die sich verwandelnde Gestalt,
die immer einsam aus dem Schicksal ragt,
die unbejubelt bleibt und unbeklagt
und unbeschrieben wie ein wilder Wald.

Du bist der Dinge tiefer Inbegriff,
der seines Wesens letztes Wort verschweigt
und sich den Andern immer anders zeigt:
dem Schiff als Küste und dem Land als Schiff.

II, 22

You are the future,
the red sky before sunrise
over the fields of time.

You are the cock's crow when night is done,
you are the dew and the bells of matins,
maiden, stranger, mother, death.

You create yourself in ever-changing shapes
that rise from the stuff of our days—
unsung, unmourned, undescribed,
like a forest we never knew.

You are the deep innerness of all things,
the last word that can never be spoken.
To each of us you reveal yourself differently:
to the ship as coastline, to the shore as a ship.

II, 22

Die Könige der Welt sind alt
und werden keine Erben haben.
Die Söhne sterben schon als Knaben,
und ihre bleichen Töchter gaben
die kranken Kronen der Gewalt.

Der Pöbel bricht sie klein zu Geld,
der zeitgemäße Herr der Welt
dehnt sie im Feuer zu Maschinen,
die seinem Wollen grollend dienen;
aber das Glück ist nicht mit ihnen.

Das Erz hat Heimweh. Und verlassen
will es die Münzen und die Räder,
die es ein kleines Leben lehren.
Und aus Fabriken und aus Kassen
wird es zurück in das Geäder
der aufgetanen Berge kehren,
die sich verschließen hinter ihm.

II, 24

The kings of the world are old and feeble.
They bring forth no heirs.

Their sons are dying before they are men,
and their pale daughters
abandon themselves to the brokers of violence.

Their crowns are exchanged for money
and melted down into machines,
and there is no health in it.

Does the ore feel trapped
in coins and gears? In the petty life
imposed upon it
does it feel homesick for earth?

If metal could escape
from coffers and factories,
and the torn-open mountains
close around it again,

we would be whole.

II, 24

Alles wird wieder groß sein und gewaltig.
Die Lande einfach und die Wasser faltig,
die Bäume riesig und sehr klein die Mauern;
und in den Tälern, stark und vielgestaltig,
ein Volk von Hirten und von Ackerbauern.

Und keine Kirchen, welche Gott umklammern
wie einen Flüchtling und ihn dann bejammern
wie ein gefangenes und wundes Tier,—
die Häuser gastlich allen Einlaßklopfern
und ein Gefühl von unbegrenztem Opfern
in allem Handeln und in dir und mir.

Kein Jenseitswarten und kein Schaun nach drüben,
nur Sehnsucht, auch den Tod nicht zu entweihn
und dienend sich am Irdischen zu üben,
um seinen Händen nicht mehr neu zu sein.

II, 25

All will come again into its strength:
the fields undivided, the waters undammed,
the trees towering and the walls built low.
And in the valleys, people as strong
and varied as the land.

And no churches where God
is imprisoned and lamented
like a trapped and wounded animal.
The houses welcoming all who knock
and a sense of boundless offering
in all relations, and in you and me.

No yearning for an afterlife, no looking beyond,
no belittling of death,
but only longing for what belongs to us
and serving earth, lest we remain unused.

II, 25

Auch du wirst groß sein. Größer noch als einer,
der jetzt schon leben muß, dich sagen kann.
Viel ungewöhnlicher und ungemeiner
und noch viel älter als ein alter Mann.

Man wird dich fühlen: daß ein Duften ginge
aus eines Gartens naher Gegenwart;
und wie ein Kranker seine liebsten Dinge
wird man dich lieben ahnungsvoll und zart.

Es wird kein Beten geben, das die Leute
zusammenschart. Du bist nicht im Verein;
und wer dich fühlte und sich an dir freute,
wird wie der Einzige auf Erden sein:
Ein Ausgestoßener und ein Vereinter,
gesammelt und vergeudet doch zugleich . . .

II, 26

You too will find your strength.
We who must live in this time
cannot imagine how strong you will become—
how strange, how surprising,
yet familiar as yesterday.

We will sense you
like a fragrance from a nearby garden
and watch you move through our days
like a shaft of sunlight in a sickroom.

We will not be herded into churches,
for you are not made by the crowd,
you who meet us in our solitude.

We are cradled close in your hands—
and lavishly flung forth.

II, 26

Es wird nicht Ruhe in den Häusern, sei's
daß einer stirbt und sie ihn weitertragen,
sei es daß wer auf heimliches Geheiß
den Pilgerstock nimmt und den Pilgerkragen,
um in der Fremde nach dem Weg zu fragen,
auf welchem er dich warten weiß.

Die Straßen werden derer niemals leer,
die zu dir wollen wie zu jener Rose,
die alle tausend Jahre einmal blüht.
Viel dunkles Volk und beinah Namenlose,
und wenn sie dich erreichen, sind sie müd.

Aber ich habe ihren Zug gesehn;
und glaube seither, daß die Winde wehn
aus ihren Mänteln, welche sich bewegen,
und stille sind wenn sie sich niederlegen—:
so groß war in den Ebenen ihr Gehn.

II, 27

There will be no rest in the houses:

                         the stir
of departure—
             someone being carried to his grave,
and another, taking up the pilgrim's staff,
to ask in unknown places for the path
where he knows you are waiting.

So many are drawn now to move toward you,
the roads are never empty.
There are so many
we can't make out their faces
or know their names,
and when they finally reach you
they are tired.

I have seen them moving like a tide.
Since then, I think the winds themselves
are stirred by the blowing of their cloaks,
and subside again when they lie down,

so great is their going across the plains.

                              II, 27

In tiefen Naechten grab ich dich, du Schatz.
Denn alle Ueberflüsse, die ich sah,
Sind Armut und armsaeliger Ersatz
Fuer deine Schöenheit, die noch nie geschah . . .

Und meine Häende, welche blutig sind
von Graben, heb ich offen in den Wind,
so daß sie sich verzweigen wie ein Baum.
Ich sauge dich mit ihnen aus dem Raum
als hättest du dich einmal dort zerschellt
in einer ungeduldigen Gebärde,
und fielest jetzt, eine zerstäubte Welt,
aus fernen Sternen wieder auf die Erde
sanft wie ein Frühlingsregen fällt.

II, 34

In deep nights I dig for you like treasure.
For all I have seen
that clutters the surface of my world
is poor and paltry substitute
for the beauty of you
that has not happened yet. . . .

My hands are bloody from digging.
I lift them, hold them open in the wind,
so they can branch like a tree.

Reaching, these hands would pull you out of the sky
as if you had shattered there,
dashed yourself to pieces in some wild impatience.

What is this I feel falling now,
falling on this parched earth,
softly,
like a spring rain?

II, 34

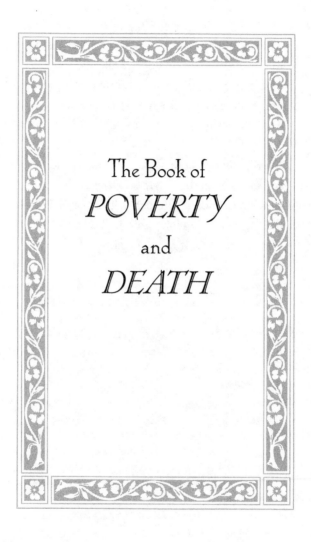

The Book of
POVERTY
and
DEATH

Vielleicht, daß ich durch schwere Berge gehe
in harten Adern, wie ein Erz allein;
und bin so tief, daß ich kein Ende sehe
und keine Ferne: alles wurde Nähe
und alle Nähe wurde Stein.

Ich bin ja noch kein Wissender im Wehe,—
so macht mich dieses große Dunkel klein;
bist Du es aber: mach dich schwer, brich ein:
daß deine ganze Hand an mir geschehe
und ich an dir mit meinem ganzen Schrein.

III, 1

It feels as though I make my way
through massive rock
like a vain of ore
alone, encased.

I am so deep inside it
I can't see the path or any distance:
everything is close
and everything closing in on me
has turned to stone.

Since I still don't know enough about pain,
this terrible darkness makes me small.
If it's you, though—

press down hard on me, break in
that I may know the weight of your hand,
and you, the fullness of my cry.

III, 1

Du Berg, der blieb da die Gebirge kamen,—
Hang ohne Hütten, Gipfel ohne Namen,
ewiger Schnee, in dem die Sterne lahmen,
und Träger jener Tale der Cyclamen,
aus denen aller Duft der Erde geht . . .

Geh ich in dir jetzt? Bin ich im Basalte
wie ein noch ungefundenes Metall?
Ehrfürchtig füll ich deine Felsenfalte,
und deine Härte fühl ich überall.

Oder ist das die Angst, in der ich bin?
die tiefe Angst der übergroßen Städte,
in die du mich gestellt hast bis ans Kinn? . . .

III, 2

You, mountain, here since mountains began,
slopes where nothing is built,
peaks that no one has named,
eternal snows littered with stars,
valleys in flower
offering fragrances of earth. . . .

Do I move inside you now?
Am I within the rock
like a metal that hasn't been mined?
Your hardness encloses me everywhere. . . .

Or is it fear
I am caught in? The tightening fear
of the swollen cities
in which I suffocate. . . .

                                        III, 2

Denn, Herr, die großen Städte sind
verlorene und aufgelöste;
. . . und ihre kleine Zeit verrinnt.

Da leben Menschen, leben schlecht und schwer,
in tiefen Zimmern, bange von Gebärde,
. . . und draußen wacht und atmet deine Erde,
sie aber sind und wissen es nicht mehr.

Da wachsen Kinder auf an Fensterstufen,
die immer in demselben Schatten sind,
und wissen nicht, daß draußen Blumen rufen
zu einem Tag voll Weite, Glück und Wind . . .

Da blühen Jungfraun auf zum Unbekannten
und sehnen sich nach ihrer Kindheit Ruh;
das aber ist nicht da, wofür sie brannten,
und zitternd schließen sie sich wieder zu.
Und haben in verhüllten Hinterzimmern
die Tage der enttäuschten Mutterschaft,
. . . und sterben lange, sterben wie in Ketten
und gehen aus wie eine Bettlerin . . .

Lord, the great cities are lost and rotting.
Their time is running out. . . .
The people there live harsh and heavy,
crowded together, weary of their own routines.

Beyond them waits and breathes your earth,
but where they are it cannot reach them.

Their children waste their days
on doorsteps, always in the same shadow.
They don't know that somewhere
wind is blowing through a field of flowers.

The young girls have only strangers to parade before,
and no one sees them truly;
so, chilled,
they close.

And in back rooms they live out the nagging years
of disappointed motherhood. Their dying is long
and hard to finish: hard to surrender
what you never received.

Dort ist der Tod . . .
der kleine Tod, wie man ihn dort begreift;
ihr eigener hängt grün und ohne Süße
wie eine Frucht in ihnen, die nicht reift.

III, 4/5

Their exit has no grace or mystery.
It's a little death, hanging dry and measly
like a fruit inside them that never ripened.

III, 4/5

O Herr, gieb jedem seinen eignen Tod.
Das Sterben, das aus jenem Leben geht,
darin er Liebe hatte, Sinn und Not.

III, 6

God, give us each our own death,
the dying that proceeds
from each of our lives:

the way we loved,
the meanings we made,
our need.

III, 6

Denn wir sind nur die Schale und das Blatt.
Der große Tod, den jeder in sich hat,
das ist die Frucht, um die sich alles dreht . . .

III, 7

For we are only the rind and the leaf.

The great death, that each of us carries inside,
is the fruit.

Everything enfolds it.

III, 7

Herr: Wir sind ärmer denn die armen Tiere,
die ihres Todes enden, wennauch blind,
weil wir noch alle ungestorben sind . . .

Denn dieses macht das Sterben fremd und schwer,
daß es nicht *unser* Tot ist; einer der
uns endlich nimmt, nur weil wir keinen reifen.
Drum geht ein Sturm, uns alle abzustreifen.

Wir stehn in deinem Garten Jahr und Jahr
Und sind die Raume, süßen Tod zu tragen;
aber wir altern in den Erntetagen,
und so wie Frauen, welche du geschlagen,
sind wir verschlossen, schlecht und unfruchtbar . . .

III, 8

Lord, we are more wretched than the animals
who do their deaths once and for all,
for we are never finished with our not dying.

Dying is strange and hard
if it is not our death, but a death
that takes us by storm, when we've ripened none within us.

We stand in your garden year after year.
We are trees for yielding a sweet death.
But fearful, we wither before the harvest.

III, 8

Ich will ihn preisen. Wie vor einem Heere
die Hörner gehen, will ich gehn und schrein.
Mein Blut soll lauter rauschen denn die Meere,
mein Wort soll süß sein, daß man sein begehre,
und doch nicht irre machen wie der Wein.

Und in den Frühlingsnächten, wenn nicht viele
geblieben sind um meine Lagerstatt,
dann will ich blühn in meinem Saitenspiele
so leise wie die nördlichen Aprile,
die spät und ängstlich sind um jedes Blatt.

Denn meine Stimme wuchs nach zweien Seiten
und ist ein Duften worden und ein Schrein:
die eine will den Fernen vorbereiten,
die andere muß meiner Einsamkeiten
Gesicht und Seligkeit und Engel sein.

III, 11

I want to praise him.
Loud as a trumpet
in the vanguard of an army,
I will run ahead and proclaim.

My words will be sweet to hear.
My people will drink them in like wine
and not get drunk.

And on spring nights, when few remain
around my tent, I will make music as soft
as northern Aprils, that hover,
late and tender, around each leaf.

So my voice becomes both a breath and a shout.
One prepares the way, the other
surrounds my loneliness with angels.

III, 11

Und gieb, daß beide Stimmen mich begleiten,
streust du mich wieder aus in Stadt und Angst.
Mit ihnen will ich sein im Zorn der Zeiten,
und dir aus meinem Klang ein Bett bereiten
an jeder Stelle, wo du es verlangst.

III, 12

May both voices accompany me,
when I am scattered again in city and fear.

They will serve me in the fury of our time
and help me make a place for you

wherever you need to be.

III, 12

Die großen Städte sind nicht wahr; sie täuschen
den Tag, die Nacht, die Tiere und das Kind;
ihr Schweigen lügt, sie lügen mit Geräuschen
und mit den Dingen, welche willig sind.

Nichts von dem weiten wirklichen Geschehen,
das sich um dich, du Werdender, bewegt,
geschieht in ihnen. Deiner Winde Wehen
fällt in die Gassen, die es anders drehen,
ihr Rauschen wird im Hin- und Wiedergehen
verwirrt, gereizt und aufgeregt . . .

III, 13

The big cities are not true; they betray
the day, the night, animals and children.
They lie with silence, they lie with noise
and with all that lets itself be used.

None of the vast events that move around you
happens there. In streets and alleys
your winds falter and churn,
and in frenzied traffic grow confused.

III, 13

Sie kommen auch zu Beeten und Alleen—:

Denn Gärten sind,—von Königen gebaut,
die eine kleine Zeit sich drin vergnügten
mit jungen Frauen, welche Blumen fügten
zu ihres Lachens wunderlichem Laut.
Sie hielten diese müden Parke wach;
sie flüsterten wie Lüfte in den Büschen,
sie leuchteten in Pelzen und in Plüschen,
und ihrer Morgenkleider Seidenrüschen
erklangen auf dem Kiesweg wie ein Bach.
Jetzt gehen ihnen alle Gärten nach—
und fügen still und ohne Augenmerk
sich in des fremden Frühlings helle Gammen
und brennen langsam mit des Herbstes Flammen
auf ihrer Äste großem Rost zusammen,
der kunstvoll wie aus tausend Monogrammen
geschmiedet scheint zu schwarzem Gitterwerk.

Und durch die Gärten blendet der Palast
(wie blasser Himmel mit verwischtem Lichte),
in seiner Säle welke Bilderlast
versunken wie in innere Gesichte,
fremd jedem Feste, willig zum Verzichte
und schweigsam und geduldig wie ein Gast.

III, 14

These winds—they come to gardens too.

There are gardens made by kings. For a time
they took pleasure there
with maidens who braided
their lovely laughter into garlands.

Like breezes through leaves
was their whispering to each other.
They glistened in their silks and furs,
and their robes rustled over the gravel paths like water.

They are gone now.
Now all gardens follow after them,
surrender and slowly burn
in the fire of autumn.
Black branches holding their flames . . .

Beyond the gardens still glimmers the palace—
bereft of festivals, paintings fading
in empty halls—silent, patient,
willing to let go.

III, 14

Dann sah ich auch Paläste, welche leben;
sie brüsten sich den schönen Vögeln gleich,
die eine schlechte Stimme von sich geben.
Viele sind reich und wollen sich erheben,—
aber die Reichen sind nicht reich.

Nicht wie die Herren deiner Hirtenvölker,
der klaren, grünen Ebenen Bewölker
wenn sie mit schummerigem Schafgewimmel
darüber zogen wie ein Morgenhimmel . . .
die dunklen Höhenzüge der Kamele
umgaben es mit der Gebirge Pracht.

Und der Geruch der Rinderherden lag
dem Zuge nach bis in den zehnten Tag,
war warm und schwer und wich dem Wind nicht aus.
Und wie in einem hellen Hochzeitshaus
die ganze Nacht die reichen Weine rinnen:
so kam die Milch aus ihren Eselinnen.

Und nicht wie jene Scheichs der Wüstenstämme,
die nächtens auf verwelktem Teppich ruhten,
aber Rubinen ihren Lieblingsstuten
einsetzen ließen in die Silberkämme.

Many are the rich who display themselves,
The palaces preen like gorgeous birds
Whose cry is a raucous screech.
But they are not truly rich.

Not rich like the nomad chieftains
whose multitudes of sheep
swept across green plains
like a morning tide;
or those whose camels moved against the sky
in majestic silhouettes.

The smell of their cattle herds
lingered, warm and heavy,
ten days after they passed.
And, as at a fine wedding, the good wine
flows the whole night through,
so ran the milk from their she-asses.

And not like the desert sheiks
who slept at night on faded carpets
but had rubies set in silver combs
to groom their favorite mares.

Und nicht wie jene Fürsten, die des Golds
nicht achteten, das keinen Duft erfand,
und deren stolzes Leben sich verband
mit Ambra, Mandelöl und Sandelholz . . .

Das waren Reiche, die das Leben zwangen
unendlich weit zu sein und schwer und warm.
Aber der Reichen Tage sind vergangen,
und keiner wird sie dir zurückverlangen,
nur mach die Armen endlich wieder arm.

III, 15

And not like those princes who found
no allurement in gold—no fragrance there—
but anointed their proud lives
with almond oil, amber, and sandalwood.

Those were riches that made life
vast and voluptuous.
Now the days of riches are gone
and no one can bring them back for us.

But we can let ourselves be poor again.

III, 15

Sie sind es nicht. Sie sind nur die Nicht-Reichen,
die ohne Willen sind und ohne Welt;
gezeichnet mit der letzten Ängste Zeichen
und überall entblättert und entstellt.

Zu ihnen drängt sich aller Staub der Städte,
und aller Unrat hängt sich an sie an.
Sie sind verrufen wie ein Blatternbette,
wie Scherben fortgeworfen, wie Skelette,
wie ein Kalender, dessen Jahr verrann,—
und doch: wenn deine Erde Nöte hätte:
sie reihte sie an eine Rosenkette und
trüge sie wie einen Talisman.

Denn sie sind reiner als die reinen Steine
und wie das blinde Tier, das erst beginnt,
und voller Einfalt und unendlich Deine
und wollen nichts und brauchen nur das Eine

so arm sein dürfen, wie sie wirklich sind.

III, 16

We are not poor. We are just without riches,
we who have no will, no world:
marked with the marks of the latest anxiety,
disfigured, stripped of leaves.

Around us swirls the dust of the cities,
the garbage clings to us.
We are shunned as if contaminated,
thrown away like broken pots, like bones,
like last year's calendar.

And yet if our Earth needed to
she could weave us together like roses
and make of us a garland.

For each being is cleaner than washed stones
and endlessly yours, and like an animal
who knows already in its first blind moments
its need for one thing only—

to let ourselves be poor like that—as we truly are.

III, 16

Du bist der Arme, du der Mittellose,
du bist der Stein, der keine Stätte hat,
du bist der fortgeworfene Leprose,
der mit der Klapper umgeht vor der Stadt . . .

Und du bist arm: so wie der Frühlingsregen,
der selig auf der Städte Dächer fällt,
und wie ein Wunsch, wenn Sträflinge ihn hegen
in einer Zelle, ewig ohne Welt.
Und wie die Kranken, die sich anders legen
und glücklich sind; wie Blumen in Geleisen
so traurig arm im irren Wind der Reisen;
und wie die Hand, in die man weint, so arm . . .

Und was sind Vögel gegen dich, die frieren,
was ist ein Hund, der tagelang nicht fraß,
und was ist gegen dich das Sichverlieren,
das stille lange Traurigsein von Tieren,
die man als Eingefangene vergaß? . . .

Du aber bist der tiefste Mittellose,
der Bettler mit verborgenem Gesicht . . .

You are the poor one, you the destitute.
You are the stone that has no resting place.
You are the diseased one
whom we fear to touch.
Only the wind is yours.

You are poor like the spring rain
that gently caresses the city;
like wishes muttered in a prison cell, without a world to
        hold them;
and like the invalid, turning in his bed to ease the pain.
Like flowers along the tracks, shuddering
as the train roars by, and like the hand
that covers our face when we cry—that poor.

Yours is the suffering of birds on freezing nights,
of dogs who go hungry for days.
Yours the long sad waiting of animals
who are locked up and forgotten.

Du bist der leise Heimatlose,
Der nichtmehr einging in die Welt;
zu gross und schwer zu jeglichem Bedarfe.
Du heulst im Sturm . . .

III, 18

You are the beggar who averts his face,
the homeless person who has given up asking;
you howl in the storm.

III, 18

Du, der du weißt, und dessen weites Wissen
aus Armut ist und Armutsüberfluß:
Mach, daß die Armen nichtmehr fortgeschmissen
und eingetreten werden in Verdruß.
Die andern Menschen sind wie ausgerissen;
sie aber stehn wie eine Blumen-Art
aus Wurzeln auf und duften wie Melissen
und ihre Blätter sind gezackt und zart.

III, 19

You who know, and whose vast knowing
is born of poverty, abundance of poverty—

make it so the poor are no longer
despised and thrown away.

Look at them standing about—
like wildflowers, which have nowhere else to grow.

III, 19

Betrachte sie und sieh, was ihnen gliche:
sie rühren sich wie in den Wind gestellt
und ruhen aus wie etwas, was man hält.
In ihren Augen ist das feierliche
Verdunkeltwerden lichter Wiesenstriche,
auf die ein rascher Sommerregen fällt.

III, 20

Look at them and see what they are like:

they move as though a wind were pushing them,
they rest as though a hand had stopped them.

In their eyes is the oncoming darkness
sweeping across summer's fields
before the storm.

III, 20

Denn sieh: sie werden leben und sich mehren
und nicht bezwungen werden von der Zeit,
und werden wachsen wie des Waldes Beeren
den Boden bergend unter Süßigkeit.

Denn selig sind, die niemals sich entfernten
und still im Regen standen ohne Dach;
zu ihnen werden kommen alle Ernten,
und ihre Frucht wird voll sein tausendfach.

Sie werden dauern über jedes Ende
und über Reiche, deren Sinn verrinnt,
und werden sich wie ausgeruhte Hände
erheben, wenn die Hände aller Stände
und aller Völker müde sind.

III, 28

There's also this to see: They will live on, they will
     increase,
no longer pawns of time.
They will grow like the sweet wild berries
the forest ripens as its treasure.

Then blessed are those who never turned away
and blessed are those who stood quietly in the rain.
Theirs shall be the harvest; for them the fruits.

They will outlast the pomp and power,
whose meanings and structures will crumble.
When all else is exhausted and bled of purpose,
they will lift their hands, that have survived.

III, 28

Nur nimm sie wieder aus der Städte Schuld,
wo ihnen alles Zorn ist und verworren
und wo sie in den Tagen aus Tumult
verdorren mit verwundeter Geduld.

Hat denn für sie die Erde keinen Raum?
Wen sucht der Wind? Wer trinkt des Baches Helle?
Ist in der Teiche tiefem Ufertraum
kein Spiegelbild mehr frei für Tür und Schwelle?
Sie brauchen ja nur eine kleine Stelle,
auf der sie alles haben wie ein Baum.

III, 29

Only retrieve them from the cities' guilt,
where everything for them is anger and confusion,
and wounded patience sucks them dry.

Has the earth, then, no room for them?
Whom does the wind seek? For whom
is the wet glistening of streams?

Is there by the banks
of the pond's deep dreaming
nowhere they can see their faces reflected?

They need only, as a tree does,
a little space in which to grow.

III, 29

Die Städte aber wollen nur das Ihre
und reißen alles mit in ihren Lauf.
Wie hohles Holz zerbrechen sie die Tiere
und brauchen viele Völker brennend auf.

Und ihre Menschen dienen in Kulturen
und fallen tief aus Gleichgewicht und Maß,
und nennen Fortschritt ihre Schneckenspuren
und fahren rascher, wo sie langsam fuhren,
und fühlen sich und funkeln wie die Huren
und lärmen lauter mit Metall und Glas.

Es ist, als ob ein Trug sie täglich äffte,
sie können gar nicht mehr sie selber sein;
das Geld wächst an, hat alle ihre Kräfte
und ist wie Ostwind groß, und sie sind klein
und ausgeholt und warten, daß der Wein
und alles Gift der Tier- und Menschensäfte
sie reize zu vergänglichem Geschäfte.

III, 31

The cities only care for what is theirs
and uproot all that's in their path.
They crush the creatures like hollow sticks
and burn up nations like kindling.

Their people serve the culture of the day,
losing all balance and moderation,
calling their aimlessness progress,
driving recklessly where they once drove slow,
and with all that metal and glass
making such a racket.

It's as if they were under a spell:
they can no longer be themselves.
Money keeps growing, takes all their strength,
and empties them like a scouring wind,
while they wait for wine and poisonous passions
to spur them to fruitless occupations.

III, 31

Und deine Armen leiden unter diesen
und sind von allem, was sie schauen, schwer
und glühen frierend wie in Fieberkrisen
und gehn, aus jeder Wohnung ausgewiesen,
wie fremde Tote in der Nacht umher;
und sind beladen mit dem ganzen Schmutze,
und wie in Sonne Faulendes bespien,—
von jedem Zufall, von der Dirnen Putze,
von Wagen und Laternen angeschrien.

Und giebt es einen Mund zu ihrem Schutze,
so mach ihn mündig und bewege ihn.

III, 32

And under these people your poor ones suffer.
All they see weighs them down,
makes them shiver and burn like a fever.
Evicted from wherever they lived,
they wander the night like ghosts,
burdened with filth and decay,
assailed by onrushing traffic,
its noise and lights

If there exists a mouth for their protection,
may it open now and speak.

III, 32

O wo ist der, der aus Besitz und Zeit
zu seiner großen Armut so erstarkte,
daß er die Kleider abtat auf dem Markte
und bar einherging vor des Bischofs Kleid.
Der Innigste und Liebendste von allen,
der kam und lebte wie ein junges Jahr;
der braune Bruder deiner Nachtigallen,
in dem ein Wundern und ein Wohlgefallen
und ein Entzücken an der Erde war . . .

III, 33

Where is he now, who leaving wealth behind
grew so bold in poverty
that he threw off his clothes before the bishop
and stood naked in the square?

The most inward and loving of all,
he came forth like a new beginning,
the brown-robed brother of your nightingales,
with his wonder and goodwill
and delight in Earth . . .

III, 33

O wo ist er, der Klare, hingeklungen?
Was fühlen ihn, den Jubelnden und Jungen,
die Armen, welche harren, nicht von fern?

Was steigt er nicht in ihre Dämmerungen—
der Armut großer Abendstern.

III, 34

Where is he, the clear one,
whose song has died away?
Do the poor, who can only wait,
feel him among them, the young and joyous one?

Does he rise for them, perhaps, at nightfall—
Poverty's evening star?

III, 34

. . . Ich danke dir, du tiefe Kraft,
die immer leiser mit mir schafft
wie hinter vielen Waenden;
jetzt ward mir erst der Werktag schlicht
und wie ein heiliges Gesicht
zu meinen dunklen Haenden.

I, 62

I thank you, deep power
that works me ever more lightly
in ways I can't make out.
The day's labor grows simple now,
and like a holy face
held in my dark hands.

I, 62

Commentary

I, 1   Our monk's cell seems to be directly under the bell tower.

The thoughts and words that were to go into *The Book of Hours* had been coming to Rilke in the mornings and evenings, as from some inner dictation. These first verses capture much of what will follow. From the start there is the conviction that our presence in the universe is part of a reciprocal process. Things need to be seen in order to be real—and so do we and so will God, whom Rilke does not yet mention here.

A third stanza, which we omitted, we translated thus:

No thing is too small for me to cherish
and paint in gold, as if it were an icon
that could bless us,
though I'll not know who else among us
will feel this blessing.

I, 2   Rilke wrote of the circles that they *"sich über die Dinge ziehn,"* literally "draw themselves over the things." Clearly what he intended was the things of this world (see the introduction).

I, 3   On a sojourn in Italy not long before, Rilke had come to love Italian painting, particularly works of the Renaissance. He and Lou Andreas-Salomé were making a study of them. As he wrote to Frieda von Bülow in August 1897: "I am especially fascinated by one Florentine master of the quattrocento— Sandro Botticelli, whom I now want to go into somewhat more deeply and personally. His Madonnas with their weary sadness, their great eyes asking for release and fulfillment . . . stand at the heart of the longing of our time" (*Letters of Rainer Maria Rilke 1892–1910*, trans. J. B. Greene and M. D. Hexter Norton. New York: W. W. Norton, 1945).

I, 4   Despite Rilke's love for Italian painting, it pales beside the evocative power of nature. The poet is ahead of his time in claiming that for conveying the sacred nothing is so appropriate as the beauty of Earth.

I, 5   As he will throughout his life and work, Rilke suggests here that we live in two dimensions at once: our immediate dramas ("sorrows and songs") and the larger context (the over-rustling tree) in which they find meaning. (See *Sonnet to Orpheus* I, ix, *In Praise of Mortality*, trans. Barrows and Macy.)

I, 6   We omitted the last seven lines, which lost the thread of the preceding image and repeated the thought that is in I, 4. After all, Rilke was writing these very quickly!

I, 7   Here is one of the many instances in *The Book of Hours* where Rilke speaks in a voice in which Eastern and Western spiritual experience converge, where emptiness (Buddhism) and devotion (Christian, and also Hindu and Sufi) come together.

I, 8   This poem, among others, made us want to translate *The Book of Hours* at this moment. What was it in the experience of this twenty-three-year-old man that allowed him such a sinister intuition of what the twentieth century would bring?

I, 9   Rilke is, of course, referring to Cain's murder of his brother Abel.

I, 10   This subtle treatment of guilt and the sensitivities that are dulled by guilt will be taken up again, but differently, when Rilke writes of the poor and oppressed in the third volume of *The Book of Hours*.

I, 11   This is one of the many poems in which Rilke departs from the popular neo-Platonist current in spirituality by honoring the dark in lieu of the light. It is exceptional in its explicit acknowledgment that darkness is the poet's very lineage. This will come to the fore in Rilke's *Sonnets to Orpheus* twenty-three years later.

I, 12 To avoid making Rilke sound too pious, we changed his "*frömmsten Gefühle*" ("most devout feelings") to "what waits within me."

I, 13 In the passage beginning, "I would describe myself," Rilke reveals a key element of his aesthetic and spiritual path, which is to place himself humbly and gratefully among the ordinary things of this world.

I, 14 The original includes the phrase: "*durch ihres / leichten Gerichts / glatte Gefühle gefürstet*," which has more nuances than English can easily convey. The lines suggest that the indifferent glide through life and rise to a princely state as a function of their lack of feeling.

I, 15 Note the juxtaposition between the construction of God, which we can carry out like good craftspeople, and an intuitive knowing. In dreams, our perception of God can be more complete.

I, 16 Creation unfolds as a natural, uncontrollable process, beyond the reaches of our will. Note the implicit contrasts here, as Rilke uses the most resistant of material elements to convey the operation of grace.

I, 17   Here, instead of deconstructing the gender, as we did in I, 5, we have changed it outright.

I, 18   For a time overfilled with words and a religion bled dry by theologizing, silence and the listening ear are, more than ever, paths to the sacred. See *Sonnet to Orpheus* I, i, "You made them, from their listening, a temple."

I, 19   This clearly follows on the previous poem. God is reassuring the one who is peering out anxiously on the beach. As Augustine said, "Thou wouldst not seek me if thou hadst not already found me."

I, 21   We have omitted six lines in the middle of this poem and a dozen at the end.

Later, in *Sonnet to Orpheus* II, viii, the childhood memory of playing ball will resurface. The ball, instead of being equated with God, as here, will signify life itself.

> *Nothing. Only the ball, the beautiful arcs it made.*
> *Not even the children were real, except for that moment*
> *Of reaching up and ah! catching the ball.*

I, 22   It is through seeing and cherishing things that Rilke resacralizes the world. "Things" includes not only artifacts, but also organic life forms, such as trees, which hold archetypal meanings of wisdom as well as fertility. A passage from a letter Rilke wrote to Ilse Jahr in 1922 elucidates the importance of this in *The Book of Hours*, and the relationships he understood among things and God and community:

"I began with things, which were the true confidants of my lonely childhood. . . . Then Russia opened itself to me and granted me the brotherliness and the darkness of God, in whom alone there is community. That was what I *named* him then, the God who had broken in upon me, and for a long time I lived in the antechamber of his name, on my knees" (*Selected Poetry*, ed. and trans. Mitchell).

I, 23 Here Rilke redeems "negative" mind states such as fear, just as he will do shortly with lust. In this he reveals a capacity for tantric play, unusual in a late-nineteenth-century Western man.

I, 25 As in mystical traditions of many faiths, Rilke uses various names and images to evoke the divine. The stunning series in this poem features some unusual ones, like home-sickness, forest, and song. The images of way and net are striking in their resonance with Buddhism.

I, 29 Rilke can love what he sees as outdated without disparaging it. He can turn and view with tenderness even our arrogance.

I, 35 Here the movement of feelings regarding death, from casual unconcern to raw fear, is similar to the movement in the German medieval mystery play *Jedermann* (*Everyman*).

I, 36 Continuing from the previous poem, circling around death, Rilke comes upon a more poignant loss. It is the loss of a relationship that is already larger than our own life.

For Rilke, we exist in part to give God something to gaze upon tenderly. Our vulnerable relationship to God is more important to Rilke than God's objective existence. As the poet wrote in a letter to his friend Mimi Romanelli in 1910:

"How far I feel this morning from the misers who, before they pray, demand to know if God exists. If he no longer exists or does not yet exist, what does it matter? It will be my prayer that will create him, for it is pure creation as it soars to the skies. And if the God my prayer projects does not persist, that's just as well: we'll make him afresh, he'll be less used up" (*Briefe*, vol. 1, *1897–1914*. Wiesbaden: Insel Verlag, 1950).

I, 38   Here, with an audacity that, for his time, is stunning, Rilke places the erotic in service to the sacred.

I, 39   As with Hindu and Sufi devotionalism, the erotic is revealed here as inseparable from our longing for God. We omitted the last six lines of the original.

I, 40   The play on contradictions, with which this poem begins, is ultimately resolved in a single image: shepherd and sheep united in their movement homeward.

I, 44   Rilke foresaw not only the apocalyptic times that have fallen upon us, but also our denial of them.

I, 45   God moves through us, as though we were doors or houses or city streets (I, 38) or forests. We, like all things, are continually being interpenetrated by God.

I, 49   This reminds us of John Donne's *Holy Sonnet* that begins: "Batter my heart, three-person'd God," and goes on to say: "I, like an usurpt town . . . / Take me to you, imprison me, for I / Except you enthrall me, never shall be free." There is a sense of fated surrender, and a deeply erotic tension.

I, 50   Taking our cue from line 7, we omitted the last two thirds of the poem.

I, 51   To a degree unusual for a Westerner, Rilke sees simultaneously the world-generating power of mind and its inherent limitations. Rilke already intuited that the spiritual journey appropriate to the twentieth century is, as Jung asserted, a journey not toward perfection, but toward wholeness.

I, 52   Rilke had beheld the dazzling onion domes of the czars only months before, on his first epochal journey to Russia. We omitted the final stanza (five lines).

I, 53   Did the poet hear these words in Schmargendorf in the early autumn of 1899, when the poems of *The Book of Hours* first began pouring out of him?

Rilke can hold together the utterly transcendent and the immanent—the God of greatest glory and the lost, forsaken one within.

See the eighth *Duino Elegy* for Rilke's moving treatment of time and timelessness, where human boundedness by time is contrasted with an animal's freer acceptance:

Where we see future,
he sees all and himself
in all, made whole for always.

I, 55   We have omitted two lines that didn't fit in the cup.

It wasn't just the first murder that fragmented God's ancient names (see I, 9), but also our presumptuous attempts to describe God. From the *Tao Te Ching*: "The Way that can be named is not the Way."

I, 59   This poem provides our preferred marching orders for the twenty-first century. Note the reciprocity of caring as we embody God and God guides us by the hand. The German echoes this relationship in the rhyme and rhythm of "*Gib mir Gewand*" (which literally means "Give me clothing," and which we have translated "Embody me") and "*Gib mir die Hand*," "Give me your hand."

I, 60   See the passage we quote from the ninth *Duino Elegy* in our introduction, and our comments on it. This poem marks a shift in *The Book of Hours*, where in Rilke's ever-deepening experience of being held by and embedded in the sacred, God becomes identified with Earth itself.

I, 61   This poem has become an anthem of the deep ecology movement, thanks to Joanna Macy in her workshops and Anita Barrows in her talks on ecopsychology.

To find the book mentioned in the last lines, look in your hands.

I, *62*   This poem, except for the last stanza, was omitted from our first edition. The childlike constancy of the poet's trust in God and his sweet discovery that it returns again and again throughout life struck us as sentimental then. That was ten years ago, when neither of us had grandchildren and the world was a less dangerous place.

II, *1*   In spite of the two-year interlude, this opening poem carries right on from the final movement of *The Book of a Monastic Life*. As God is recognized as Earth, so are we, invited to go out into the world as into our own hearts. Similarly, we are urged not only to find sacredness in things, but also to become a thing ourselves, and to ripen until we are real.

Of all the seasons, Rilke most loved autumn. He found it released his creative powers.

II, *2*   Already, in 1901, Rilke prefigures the broken faces of Picasso, and also the toxic tides and intrauterine contaminations of the century's end.

II, *3*   See I, 25, "you dark net threading through us." See also the first words of the *Duino Elegies*: "If I cried out, who/ in the hierarchies of angels/ would hear me?" These more famous lines written in 1922 take up the questioning Rilke is doing in the sixth stanza here.

II, *4*   Rilke really did say "inside me": this is not Barrows and Macy reconstructing gender! Rilke sees us all as pregnant with the future, pregnant with God.

II, 5   See the introduction. Rilke wrote these poems while awaiting the birth of his child and while afflicted with domestic worries. His sense of alienation from his own father must have been aroused.

II, 6   Rilke was very strongly influenced by Nietzsche, through Lou; but to Rilke it's only the Big Daddy God who is dead. Rilke's relationship with his own father, an ambitious but failed military man, was a source of great suffering to the poet. Rilke senior had little understanding of his son's life choices, and did not approve of them.

II, 9   Rilke's father died in March 1906, three months after the publication of *The Book of Hours*. What Rilke inherited came not from his parents so much as from Russia and Italy, from Lou and Rodin, from humanity's history and art.

II, 10   Here again, the ninth *Duino Elegy* is prefigured (see the introduction).

II, 7   No, this is not a misnumbering. We have altered Rilke's ordering of the poems so as not to interrupt the sequence that immediately precedes and which seems all of a piece. This poem, which was written in 1897, was originally addressed not to God but to Lou. Rilke slipped it under her door in the cottage where they had their first and greatest passionate idyll. Until their publication in 1905, Lou was the only person to whom Rilke showed the poems of *The Book of Hours*.

II, 11   We have omitted the poem's first eight lines. The portion we translated recalls for us the palace museums in Munich, exhibiting old carriages and belongings of a long-gone royal family. It was largely from and for this grand outmoded culture that our masks were fashioned.

From Rilke's journal, November 3, 1899: "The sense people have of impermanence and perishing comes mostly from their own not-having-been-ness [*Nichtgewesen-sein*]. In order to be, it is not enough to be born" (*Tagebücher aus der Frühzeit*. Frankfurt: Insel Verlag, 1942).

II, 12   The shift here in sense of agency—even who the agent is—bespeaks the experience of grace. As in the development of the ecological self we realize that we are "being lived" by a vaster power and from a deeper source than our separate ego.

II, 15   Again the mystic speaks to the theologian, saying: "Be still and know."

We have translated *Gesetze* as both "Ways" (I, 25) and "laws." Unusual in a mystic is how Rilke appreciates the lawful unfolding of the Way. This is close to the Buddhist meaning of Dharma.

II, 16   Here the request that Rilke made of God in the previous poem is illustrated. This is the kind of law he meant: it is not commandments from a jealous, judging God, but the coherent causal patterns that manifest the creative intelligence of Earth.

II, 19   Soon Rilke, too, would leave the home he had made with his wife and baby daughter in Westerwede. His poetry was at stake; but while he felt forced to flee the narrow confines of domesticity, he maintained a lifelong friendship with Clara Westhoff and loyally promoted her artistic work.

II, 22   We translated "*Inbegriff*" as "innerness"; the literal sense is "inner meaning."

   Note how Rilke links the future with the innermost part of our being, like a seed we carry within us. Although Rilke intuits the oncoming darkness and unprecedented suffering the century will bring, he also affirms—and in this there is profound hopefulness—the organic ripening of our true nature.

II, 24   Here Rilke speaks in the great ongoing tradition of poets such as Dante and Neruda who take on the political and economic realities of their time. Rilke conveys the exhaustion of political will and the profound loss of vitality resulting from the growing power of industrial capital.

II, 25   This follows directly on the preceding poem, with a striking shift to a major key. Rilke sees that our freeing ourselves from the power of money does not mean fleeing what is material. We seek not to transcend the things of this world, but to learn to care for them more deeply.

II, 26   Note the dialectic in our relationship with God. Like all mystics, we know the divine through our solitude; yet our sharing of that knowing strengthens our experience of community.

II, 27   Pilgrimage, which furnishes the title to this book, and which was suggested from its first poem, now becomes explicit. Whereas in the poem about the force of the storm (II, 1) we are called into our own vast loneliness, here it is also made clear that pilgrimage is a collective endeavor.

The true experience of community is not in staying with the status quo, but in moving forth together, in response to a summons, toward a future that cannot yet be envisioned.

II, 34 Perhaps the pilgrimage we are making is not so much to redeem ourselves as to retrieve God.

We omitted the middle section of the poem, which employs a different metaphor:

> But the way to you is terribly far,
> hard to make out, overgrown.
> No one has walked it for a long time.
> How lonely you are—
> you are loneliness itself,
> dear heart drifting into distant valleys.

III, 1 Donald Prater, in his excellent biography of Rilke (*A Ringing Glass.* Oxford: Clarendon Press, 1986), says that this poem was prompted by Rilke's claustrophobia in the train tunnels through the Alps on his way to Viareggio.

III, 2 A contemporary note is struck here, as the poet experiences that the distress of urban civilization is something he carries inside him. The anguish he witnessed in Paris is present as he speaks of "the swollen cities."

III, 4/5 We have combined most of 4 with the last lines of 5. The two themes of this book, poverty and death, emerge together.

The tragedy of the urban poor is reflected in their being deprived of even the ground in which to grow a meaningful death.

III, 6   Our living includes our dying.

III, 7   Our living grows our dying organically. These are the first several of seventeen lines in the original—what we felt to be the core.

III, 8   Again we have harvested the fruit, this time from an original of twenty-eight lines.

III, 11   This poem of praise bursts in with an exuberance of energy ranging from shout to whisper. There is resilience in the poet's capacity to call down blessings in such a variety of settings.

III, 12   The original this time is actually as brief as our translation. Both these voices are within every one of us, and needed now, scattered as we are "in city and fear."

III, 13   Not only are the cities lost (III, 4/5), but within them the very forces of nature become obscured.

III, 14   The first line here comes at the end of the previous poem. We include it with this one because it announces its theme.

III, 15   We omitted thirteen lines. In this poem is a celebration of sensory wealth rare for a northern European.

III, *16, 18, 19* Rilke was sometimes accused of romanticizing poverty. Indeed we have omitted several cloying passages. Yet the poet's anguish in beholding the poor was genuine. Describing his experience in Paris, he wrote later to Lou Andreas-Salomé:

"O Lou, I was so tormented day after day. For I understood all those people, and although I went around them in a wide arc, they had no secret from me. I was torn out of myself into their lives, through all their burdened lives" (*Letters*, trans. Greene and Norton).

III, *20* This is another of Rilke's prophetic poems.

III, *28* For Rilke the sense of the future remains strong. No horror of the present can excise the fact that tomorrow will dawn and that change is constant. The lawfulness in nature that he has celebrated in earlier poems here supports his confidence that goodness will not die.

III, *29* Just as Rilke sees God in nature, so would he have the poor find themselves there.

III, *31* Here Rilke's compassion for the oppressed shifts into a blistering indictment of the industrial growth system. It drives into madness the very ones who serve it and imagine they benefit from it.

III, *32* In directing our attention to the plight of the poor, Rilke himself becomes the prophetic voice he calls for.

III, *33* Rilke's evocation of St. Francis captures *il poverello*'s audacity as much as his tenderness for all creation.

III, *34* St. Francis becomes in these lines one more evidence of the sacred in nature, which Rilke has celebrated from the beginning of *The Book of Hours*.

I, *62* This stanza closed the last poem we translated from *The Book of a Monastic Life*. We place it here because it provides a simple and reverent closure for the whole work.